LOST IN AMERICA

LOST IN AMERICA

A Journey with My Father

SHERWIN B. NULAND

ALFRED A. KNOPF   NEW YORK   2003

THIS IS A BORZOI BOOK
PUBLISHED BY ALFRED A. KNOPF

Copyright © 2003 by Dr. Sherwin B. Nuland

www.aaknopf.com

Portions of the prayer Untaneh Tokef were adapted from
Mahzor for Rosh Hashanah and Yom Kippur by Rabbi Jules Harlow
(Rabbinical Assembly, 1972); *Mahzor Hadash* by Rabbi Sidney
Greenberg and Rabbi Jonathan Levine (Prayer Book Press, 1977);
and *Mahzor le-Rosh ha-Shanah ule-Yom ha-Kippurim* by Rabbi
Morris Silverman (Prayer Book Press, 1951).

Library of Congress Cataloging-in-Publication Data
Nuland, Sherwin B.
Lost in America : a journey with my father /
Sherwin B. Nuland.—1st ed.
p. cm.
ISBN 0-375-41294-8
1. Nuland, Sherwin B. 2. Nuland, Sherwin B.—Family relationships.
3. Nudelman, Meyer. 4. Jews—New York (N.Y.)—Biography. 5. Bronx
(New York, N.Y.)—Biography. 6. Father and child. I. Title.
F128.9.J5 N85 2003
974.7'275004924—dc21
2002040795

Manufactured in the United States of America

Published January 17, 2003

Reprinted Once

Third Printing, March 2003

To Vittorio—
Because of you, it became possible

To Sarah—
Because of you, it became real

Be kind, for everyone you meet is fighting a great battle.

Attributed to PHILO OF ALEXANDRIA

Introduction

We stood there at the foot of the grave, just the two of us—shoulder to shoulder, father to son, generation to generation. An aura of memories enveloped us. Those old and those more recent, those bidden and those unbidden, all alike crowded into that moment of our lives, as they always do when my elder son and I stand together in that greenswarded place of the dead. Here thousands and more thousands of closely planted headstones mark the burial sites of turn-of-the-twentieth-century Jewish immigrants and their descendants.

Drew and I were standing before the grave of my father, now dead some forty years and yet in some ways more commanding and more needful than he had been during his life. Hundreds of yards away, an occasional workman could be seen attending to some cluster of ivy or an unruly growth of bush, but it was too early on that crisp October morning for anyone else to have yet arrived. Except for our quiet conversation, the only sounds interrupting the verdant stillness were the chirping of birds and the occasional roar of a low-flying airplane going to or from Kennedy Airport, where my son had arrived from half a world away less than an hour earlier. In that section of the entire sprawling metropolis of long-mourned or forgotten lives, Drew and I were by ourselves. We were alone with our dead.

Drew has accompanied me here since he was a small boy, in recent years planning his journeys from the far-off country where he lives, to stand with me on my yearly pilgrimages to this place. Though he never knew any of those with whose memories we come to commune—my father, my mother, Aunt Rose, and a baby brother who died before I was born—they have made their mark on him just as surely as though he had grown up among them in that small Bronx apartment of such emotional turbulence. But none of them has affected his life more than my father.

On these visits, Drew is the surrogate for all of my children, who knowingly or not accompany me on a circuitous journey toward an attempt at understanding that I began long before any of them were born. It is a journey that can never be completed. I am trying to find the truth of my father, and in the process to find a part of myself that I have never understood. But like the countless others who have embarked on similar quests, I am determined to travel as far as I can toward the ultimate destination.

We visit our dead to keep faith with them. But much more difficult is making the peace that so many of us have never achieved. It is a kind of peace that can be found only when we come to terms with just who it is that they really were, and who it is that we ourselves have become, so much of it because of them.

My father's power and the weakness that nurtured it have accompanied me all the days of my life. I have struggled to be the un-him—to be the opposite of what he was—and in the struggling I have faltered and fallen many times. His lingering power over me has been the source of much of my weakness; I have responded to the threat of his weakness by seeking to find ways to resist it—to be so powerful against it that I am unassailable by that great portion of himself that he has left within me. And in the process, I have instead become rather more like him than less.

I am writing this book to help me come to terms with my father. I am writing this book to finally make peace with him, and perhaps with myself.

LOST IN AMERICA

I

I have never read a single textbook paragraph on the subject of depression. I have never looked at a sentence written in later tranquillity by a recovered sufferer. I do not need to learn about depression from the pages of a book. I have had my own.

The solitary torment of a depressed mind eludes any attempt to make it apprehensible to those who have not experienced it. And even for those of us who have endured those desolate months or years, no matter the generalized similarities of the depression, each of us has suffered uniquely, and alone. Neither vivid description nor the empathy of others can pierce the darkness of the long night.

And yet, after depression lifts, it can only be remembered but not retrieved—thank God it cannot be retrieved! Just as physical pain loses its intense reality once it has been eased, the anguish of profound melancholia evades even the most determined attempts at clear perception when its dreadful grip has relaxed. It goes to some underplace where it can be seen through a glass, darkly—but not face-to-face. Depression resists being called up again, unless its own tortured purposes determine that a proper time has come to exert authority once more. Then, enveloping reason in a foreboding of ill, its all-pervasive fog rolls back in as though it had never left, to suffocate undisturbed thought in its own terrifying, familiar way. Could a recurrence of depression give itself voice, it would speak in the muffled and mocking tones of a vengeful enemy.

It is not my purpose here to describe my depression or to make it palpable to others. Instead, I have a different intent. I am trying to return to memory; perhaps memory can fill the empty places in my understanding, and bring me closer to the entire truth about my life.

From my late thirties until my early forties, I underwent a period of depression that gradually deepened into an intensity so absolute that I finally required admission to a mental hospital, where I stayed for more than a year. Neither medication, psychotherapy, the determined efforts of friends nor the devotion of the few people whose love never deserted me had even the most minimal beneficial effect on my worsening state of mind. Finally, faced with my resistance to all forms of treatment till then attempted, the senior psychiatrists at the institution in which I was confined recommended the draconian measure of lobotomy. Their justification for such a drastic course was that disrupting the brain's neural pathways might bring an immediate end to the complex of obsessional thinking and behavior to which I had succumbed.

I was, in fact, completely disabled by pathological preoccupations and fears. Obsession with coincidences; fixations on recurrent numbers; feelings of worthlessness and physical or sexual inadequacy; religious anxieties of guilt and concerns about God's will; ritualistic thinking and behavior—they crowded in on one another so forcefully as to occupy every lacuna of my mind. I cowered before them, not only emotionally but physically, too—my hunched-over posture reflected my decline into helplessness. Rational thinking was driven out by a ferocity of fear that consumed all energy and pride. I came not to have a moment's peace from the din and deluge of that rampaging stampede of obsessional ideations. So profound was my depression and so tyrannical the jumble of unbidden thoughts and compulsive actions that they ruled the hours of my days and the days of my years. I feared the obsessions, I feared the threatening loss of control, and I feared the fear—all at once. Mostly, I feared for my sanity.

Each day began in the same way. Month after month after tortured month, I would awaken early—very early, usually before 4:00 a.m.—in the blissful certainty that I had miraculously become well. For no longer than a fraction of a second, which seemed like an hour spent in some Edenic garden of normal health, I was my old self, gratefully free of the suffocating heaviness at the bottom of that vortex in which I had been trapped until the release brought by sleep the night before. The healing interlude of oblivion had elevated me to a freedom high above the turbulent depths into which I had been plunged. Awakening in that precious eyeblink of tranquil time, I looked down from the height of liberation and wondered how I could have let myself become entrapped in such foolishness as mental disease. And then, abruptly, the brief golden escape would always terminate, as though it had never been. Reality thundered back, and I was thrown down once again into the swirling maelstrom of obsessions as the ferocious fear returned.

And with it came other unwelcome intruders, too. The unrelenting anguish of frenzied thoughts was reflected in an actual physical heaviness in the center of my chest, as though my heart had become overburdened with the expanding fullness of the tumult within. There were times, not only at that early-morning hour but during the day as well, when I had to grasp my senses tightly in order to keep my wildly racing mind from shattering into fragments that might be thrown violently into a centrifugal dispersion of madness from which there could be no return. Even today, when I look at Edvard Munch's *The Scream* and recognize the horror depicted there, I understand it in a way that I would gladly abandon in return for my previous ignorant inability to perceive its full meaning.

But through it all—and it does seem incomprehensible as I look back on it—I somehow never lost the capacity to separate some remaining crystal-clear perception of true thought from the parasitic malevolences that had achieved dominion over me. Even at the worst of the chaos, I seemed always to retain an image of my inner ogre as it looked when I could distance myself from it, and to recognize it as a stranger from whom it should be possible to separate. But in spite of that perception, I could somehow not manage to free myself from the interloper's awful infiltration. It was as though the reflective, self-assured man I had always believed myself to be had only to will the invader out. But I was unable to do it. An overmastering power had become the occupier of my soul. And yet, I remained determined to defeat it.

I was saved from the drastic intervention of lobotomy by the refusal of the twenty-seven-year-old resident psychiatrist assigned to my case to agree with his teachers. He dug in his heels and would not allow the operation to be done, threatening to resign if he was overruled. He was a young man highly regarded in that place, and he was stubborn. At his insistence, a course of elec-troshock therapy was reluctantly embarked upon.

I would learn much later that virtually everyone familiar with my case despaired of the possibility of recovery. I had become notorious in that place as the deeply depressed surgeon chained by obsessions of such awful power that they yielded to nothing. On the entire sprawling campus on which stood the numerous build-ings of the psychiatric hospital, only the troubled surgeon and his resident doctor continued to believe that he could get well.

At first, the newly instituted treatment made not a whit of dif-ference. The number of electroshock treatments mounted, but still no improvement took place. The total would eventually reach twenty. Somewhere around the middle of the course, a glimmer of change made itself evident, which encouraged the skeptical staff to continue a series of treatments they had begun only to mollify a promising young man in training.

In the beginning only a bit but after a while more palpably, the depression began to lighten and the obsessions became less insistent. As inexplicable as it seems, I sometimes forgot to think about them entirely. In time, I was sleeping until a normal hour each morning, and I would wake thinking clearly and remaining optimistic for most of the day. The act of will that had seemed impossible of fulfillment now came within reach, and finally in a single surge of determination, I made it happen.

I still wonder at the scene, which I remember so clearly. One Sunday morning in January 1974, I was standing alone in the little kitchen of the residence unit where I lived with some fifteen other patients, thinking very calmly—analytically, in fact—about the content of my galaxy of pathological ideations. It crossed my mind that it was no longer necessary to give in to them each time one or another would flash into consciousness. Why not figuratively turn away and refuse to succumb? Why not respond to their pernicious urgings with some dismissive formula, like "Ah, fuck it"? As recently as a month earlier, I could not have entertained such a notion, so tightly was I being held in the grip of those iron chains of agitated depression. Until then, rejecting an obsessional thought had only stoked anxiety, but on that morning, release seemed for the very first time achievable. I felt like a child who has matured just enough so that he no longer has to avoid stepping on sidewalk cracks.

Then and there, I resolved to abandon my pathological limitations in a single determined stroke. It was as though the electroshock had burned away a tightly coiled network intertwined in my brain, constricting free will. And it had also incinerated so much of my recent memory that most of the relatively new reminders to think dangerous thoughts went with it. I knew even then that my short-term memory would in time return, but I was now finally able to confront the remaining obsessional patterns and do with them what I would. I walked out of that small room without coil or chains, armed with the slogan of "Ah, fuck it!" My sea of troubles had receded.

And so, I recovered. I recovered so well, in fact, that in the four remaining months of hospitalization, I lost all but the dimmest memory of the obsessions and saw my depression disappear entirely.

Through the worst and darkest days, I had been sustained by the indistinguishable certainty that in some way, I knew not how, I would find my way back to health. And I was sustained also by love. My brother, Harvey, had refused to believe that he would have to surrender me to my sickness. But beyond anything else, I was sustained by the intensity of the love I bore for my two children, Toria and Drew. In the midst of the most profound despondency and the severest of the obsessions, I had only to open the drawer of the small desk in my room and stare for a few moments at a large photograph of the two of them, as though it were an amulet of faith. So long as I had that picture and those children, I never stopped believing that I would in time emerge from the blackness of despair.

When I left the hospital, I was forty-three years old, divorced, and—thanks to the illness and my former wife's lawyer—without money or property. Life began anew. As though in recompense for my losses, I was granted the miracle of the woman who is now my wife, Sarah, and we began to build a life together. In due course, we had two more children, Will and Molly, to share it with us, along with the two older kids, who had by then come to live with us. We were a family of six. All but small bits of my memory had returned, and I was able to resume my surgical practice.

For seventeen years, I was free of any hint of depression. But in the past decade, I have had a few recurrences, though none remotely approaching the catastrophe of thirty years ago, and none accompanied by more than a whiff of obsessional thinking. When the old pain begins to make its presence known, I return to the wisdom—and the presence—of that former psychiatric resident who saved my life and my sanity. He has become as my brother. He needs no pill or potion to help me. There is only the voice that I long ago came to trust, because it guides me gently back to the fullness of myself.

But memory plays tricks. It has its own plans, and goes its own way. Sometimes it withholds key elements in the story of a life. They may never be divulged, or they may come to the surface only when the mind is prepared to receive them. And perhaps that is why no mention of my father—except in obliquities—is to be found in any book I have previously written. So far from deliberate was his absence from my pages that I was shocked when it was pointed out to me soon after *How We Die* was published, in 1994. But I knew immediately what to make of it. Unlike any of the others whose devotion has brought me to this place and this time, my father—now dead more than forty years—remains a constant looming presence in everything I do, but an unresolved one.

He walks with me through every day of my life, in that unsteady, faltering gait that so embarrassed me when I was a boy. Always, he is holding fast to the upper part of my right arm. Now and then, the uncertain grip of his hand slips just a bit and he grabs more deeply for security onto the cloth of my sleeve and the skin beneath. It is pinched between his fingertips as though in the jaws of a clamp, and I wince with pain. As his hold tightens, I tell him that he is hurting me. He is offended by that, and lets me know it in grumbling Yiddish.

As we make our way together, my father—I called him Daddy when I was small, because it sounded American and that is how he

so desperately wanted things to seem—is speaking in the idiosyncratic rhythms of a self-constructed English pronounced in a way
that emanated from no one's lips but his, a particularistic accent that
is better described as having been Yiddishoid than Yiddish, infil-
trated as it was with the speech mannerisms of the Italian-born
garment workers with whom he toiled in the sweatshops of New
York's Garment District. I have never heard anyone speak that way,
either in terms of pronunciation or sentence structure. Try as I may,
it defies my attempts to imitate it or reproduce it on the page. Like
everything else about my father, his speech was one of a kind. As
paradoxical as it seems to invoke such a term when describing a virtually unassimilated Jewish immigrant who knew nothing about the
wider culture of this or any other country—who was, in fact, lost in
America—Meyer Nudelman was sui generis, in a class by himself.

But there was nothing sui generis about his appearance. He
was of average height for his generation of shtetl Jews (which is to
say about five-foot-seven), and his head of fine dark hair formed a
widow's peak above a high forehead. If there is truly such a thing
as a Jewish nose, Meyer Nudelman was its proprietor. Centered on
a broad, straight nasal bone that widened at the cartilage, its nos-
trils flared into a classical Semitic curve on each side. His eyes were
deep brown in color, with just a touch of world-weary sadness.
They were covered always with a barely perceptible tear layer, the
slightly glistening effect being one of soulful musing at all that they
had seen, and were seeing. He had a way of laughing uncontrollably when something struck him as being particularly funny, which
made those soulful eyes fill with tears. As a boy, I would sometimes have to ask him whether he was laughing or crying, which
could be very perilous if the episode was the result of a facetious
barb I had just thrown in his direction. Like so many other things
about him, his responses to such wisecracks were unpredictable—
sometimes he loved a joke on himself, and sometimes he reacted
with outrage.

Meyer's eyes were among the several physical characteristics that set him apart from the rest of our family. Ours were blue, and every one of us had hair that, if not still blond, was identifiable as having been that color in youth. We were clear-eyed and looked optimistic in spite of ample reason to be otherwise.

Not only his eyes and the color of his hair made Meyer seem different. He was as unsure of his movements as he was unsure of his place in our family. I would later learn, in medical school, that a diffuse scarring of the spinal cord resulting from an infection acquired in his youth had left him progressively unable to use his hands or legs in the unthinking, automatic way that other people do. His condition worsened each year I knew him. He had to concentrate his mind on every step and every movement, even when he brought a forkful of food to his mouth. Something of him had retreated to a deep place within, and he showed it by a stoop in his back and a hunching of his shoulders. It was this posture that I assumed during the worst of my illness.

A proud man reduced to debility is hypersensitive to any perceived slight. My father demanded not merely deference but total respect from his two sons, and when he thought it not to be forthcoming, he would lash out in a ranting deluge of anger that had more in it of impotent rage than of authority. A look, a word, even a suspect intonation from either of us or some other member of the family was enough to incite his wrath.

By the time of my adolescence, my father had become so disabled by that seemingly undiagnosable neurological disease that he needed help in some of his daily activities, particularly walking. If there was even a bit of snow or ice on the sidewalks, he could make his way only with great difficulty. Walking to the subway station each morning in order to get to work, he would clutch my arm tightly as we laboriously negotiated the three long blocks. At the end of the day, I always waited for him at the 183rd Street station, just beyond the turnstiles. He would appear promptly at 5:45, furious if he did not see me standing in my usual place as he approached. The difficult trudge homeward took fifteen minutes, more or less, depending on the accumulation of snow and ice. I had to take him to many other places, too—my right arm was his staff. I could advance only slowly, because he held me back; I could wander only so far, because there were times when I needed to be available for him. Even now, I can feel his hand squeezing my arm. I am in his grip still.

In the very fabric of my father's power over me lay his power-lessness, and his need for my power. His hold did not signify strength, but weakness. His weakness was his strength. I did his bidding, always fearful of being the agent of his destruction if I did otherwise—always fearful, too, of the explosiveness of his wrath. And in this, he was my imperious overlord. I would only be free with his death, or so I thought.

I would be proven wrong. With his death came a new power, with far greater consequences than those I had grown up with. It was the smothering power of enduring love, and, though I refused to face it for decades to come, enduring hate. I have been able to do nothing that might permanently free me from either; nor have I been able to do anything that might free me from my father and his awful power over me. Perhaps now I have begun to see that it is not freedom I should have been seeking, but understanding.

II

My father does not actually appear in my earliest memory of him. But the threat of his furious anger looms over the series of moments even as they are recalled.

It is in the form of single still images that I remember him from those early years. Each picture is preserved as though a camera had caught a series of lifetime's memories in individual blinks of an eye. Sometimes, an image is followed by a brief cinematic flow of film, but rarely more. And always a distinct emotion or mood is brought back to my mind when the pictures appear.

It is midafternoon and I have just spied Daddy's pocket watch and chain on a small table alongside the living-room couch. The sight of the inexpensive silvery timepiece attached to a flat strand of worn and tarnished links is particularly attractive because its imperious owner has recently scolded me for daring to play with it. I pick up the entire clump of watch and chain. In the next remembered picture, I have made my way to the electric outlet on the nearest wall, and I am staring at it, as though trying to make a decision. Stabilizing myself on chubby knees, I stuff several links of the chain into one of the outlet's parallel slits.

With a sudden roaring wallop, a colossal burst of sparks and energy blasts up out of the wall as a paralyzing vibratory surge of electricity courses through every part of me and lifts my helpless body momentarily off the floor. Hearing my shrieking wail, terrified Momma flies out of some other room, screaming, no doubt certain that I have been killed. She gathers me up and I submerge myself into her softness. We are both weeping. She croons a gentle, familiar reassurance, but I am hysterical.

The pervasive feeling hovering over these horrifying images is not the sudden fright, but a sense of foreboding: Something more is yet to come, and in its own way it will be as threatening as the terror I have just survived.

My mind has stored no memory of what actually happened when my father came home that evening. But the recalled sense of apprehension makes me certain that it must have been similar to later such episodes. Momma would not even have the choice not to tell her husband of the afternoon's near cataclysm.

Once informed, my father would have unleashed a thunder of abuse at Momma, an explosion of fury not less startlingly instantaneous than the blasting electric shock that had almost taken my life. A baritone roar of infuriated, eye-flashing Yiddish invective must have pounded her remorse with an unrelenting hammer of accusation, as though Daddy was convinced that she had neglected me and thereby demeaned him by undermining his ability to protect us; as though he himself was therefore the injured party; as though the accident was somehow a breach of his authority over the family and even a rejection of the love he never quite knew how to express. Very likely, it was days before he uttered a kind word—or perhaps any word at all—to her. I would see this pattern played out again and again in the coming years.

Why is my remembrance of that electric shock always accompanied by the looming sense of worse to come? How can I be so sure about my father's rage on that day? Is it really possible that at two and a half I could already have learned to anticipate such an excessive response, or am I looking back on the entire episode reflected in the mirror of so many subsequent paroxysms of self-righteous outrage?

The truth is not to be known. The only certainty is that the remembered sequence of images from that terrifying afternoon almost seventy years ago is inseparable from the dread of my father's coming rage; it is inseparable from the sense that Momma and I cowered in anticipation of its outburst just as we would cower in the torrential force of my father's wrath when it finally came.

Looking back on my earliest remembered years, I see my parents far less as a couple than as the sources of two quite disparate emotions—emotions of golden safety with one and sporadic danger with the other. They originated from Momma, who lived only for me, and Daddy, who never quite understood how to be my father.

There was a magic about being with Momma. The magic was at its greatest when we were together and safe—when no harshness was invading the encirclement of blessedness in which I imagined her to move. Momma was the totality of all I knew to be good, and I was certain that she lived only to be my mother. She was to be shared with no one. Whatever others might require of her was only a transient distraction until she could return to me, a little boy certain that he was her reason for being.

Like all mothers, mine was beautiful. My now-aging gaze often turns to a small collection of photographs from her teen years, which were spent on my grandmother's Connecticut farm, and I see a wistful young woman with gently smiling eyes and high Slavic cheekbones. Above the graceful curve of a wide forehead, her light-colored hair piles thickly on her head, arcing back toward a combed bun, in the style of the time. She looks kind, and though no older than seventeen, she already looks wise. In pictures taken in much later years, she has become just a bit heavy—and tired, always seeming tired and, in objective terms, no longer beautiful. The burden of painful years changed her. She has become an almost plump middle-aged Jewish housewife. But the kindness and the wisdom are still in those wistful blue eyes.

Our family lived in a part of the South Bronx now so changed that only traces of it remain. The heavily traveled Cross Bronx Expressway is today the dominant feature of a congested area that was once our quiet neighborhood. At that time—the early 1930s—the entire landscape for miles around was a wide-open expanse of untended fields, interrupted by streets of scattered one- and two-family homes that broke up what was otherwise a sparsely settled flatland called Unionport. So distant from the city in geography and spirit was this eastward reach of the Bronx that the Archdiocese of New York considered it sufficiently remote to have built a large orphan asylum there, called the Catholic Protectory. The area was also home to two rather disparate sources of odor, a pig farm and a perfume factory. The first had at one time been owned by a man named West, which led to the irony that this eastern region of New York City was called West Farms. Very likely, the factory producing cheap perfume had been built in that location because its sickening, sweetish afflation would not have been tolerated in a more populated or prosperous area. The stench of West's pigs came and went with the prevailing winds, but the cloying smell of the perfumery was always with us.

Somewhere near the middle of that diverse expanse of open land was Olmstead Avenue, one of several crisscrossing streets broken up by scattered groups of small wooden homes and an occasional two-story brick house, set at varying distances from one another. Large empty tracts of neglected, weed-covered land filled the surrounding acres.

Two or three small stores were clustered on each side of the north corner of one of the few blocks that constituted the entire length of Olmstead Avenue. North of them, in the middle of the block, a lone four-story brick house had been built. The high number assigned to 1215 Olmstead Avenue gave the impression that it lay on some long and bustling boulevard, but like the name of the local trolley-car stop, it was misleading. The structure's distinction consisted of being the only apartment building visible as far as the eye could see. It was of such a construction and appearance that it would be called a tenement were it surrounded by a cluster of houses just like it. But 1215 escaped that opprobrium by standing aloof and alone in that wide landscape, and also by being free of the city fire code's requirement that buildings of five or more stories be festooned with fire escapes.

In the small first-floor flat fronting on the street lived Meyer and Vitsche (referred to as Violet when a formal purpose demanded it) Nudelman and their two boys, Harvey and Sherwin, or, as we were always called in the household, Hershel and Shepsel, or Sheppy. Living with us were Momma's widowed mother—my Bubbeh—and her unmarried sister, Aunt Rose, or Tante Aya, as Harvey, for some unknown reason, had labeled her when he was barely able to speak. Around the corner, my mother's other sister, Tante Beattie, and her husband, Uncle Manny Ritter (a Jew born in Austria, and therefore in his own way also an anomaly among us), rented the lower floor of a two-family house, where they lived with their daughter, Elke Dveyreh, or Arline.

We were a family of immigrants, even the two of us born in America. Yiddish was the language of the household, and the worldview of the ghettoized Jews of Russia pervaded the spoken and unspoken teachings transmitted to Harvey and me. None of the adults ever learned to read or write any English beyond their own painstaking signatures. What they knew of the daily world came from the radio and the Yiddish press, and, in time, from their boys.

Bubbeh spoke no English at all, though she had been living in New York for almost three decades. She had arrived in this country in 1903, to join her husband and two sons, both around twenty years old, who had preceded her by some three years from the small city of Novaradugk in the northern Pale of Russia. She brought her four daughters with her, expecting, like so many others, to find the miracle of this golden land awaiting her. Instead, she was greeted by her three men already in the advanced stages of tuberculosis. One by one, within a few years, each of them would die, as would her eldest daughter, during childbirth, not much more than a decade later. America, the land of abundance, had provided her with an abundance of sorrow; America, the land that promised bounty to come, had not kept its promise. Instead, the nation of opportunity stole her dreams and returned them tear-stained and desolate.

A tough-minded and even dictatorial woman of fierce independence in her youth and middle years, Bubbeh had held sway as the acknowledged leader of a large and extended family since her husband and two sons had died. She had been matriarch, counsel, and adopted aunt—Tante Peshe, as she was universally called—to several generations of Russian-born men and women, some of them scarcely younger than she. She advised, she granted permission, and she forbade—and everyone did her bidding. She had held court for decades, but her dominion was already much weakened by the time Harvey, Arline, and I appeared in her life. Age, misfortune, and the simple passage of time, which brought self-sufficiency to so many of those for whom she was a source of strength—all of these factors had done their work. Bubbeh was a four-foot-ten-inch timeworn woman of seventy-eight when I was born, and the fight and power had long since gone out of her.

Bubbeh's Yiddish was the sound of home. It was the language in which we spoke to her, the language that Jews have for centuries called *mammaloschen,* the tongue spoken by mothers. To us, it was *Bubbehloschen.* I heard it as a soft Litvak that caressed a child's ear with the gentle reassurance of changelessness, even as everything was changing around both of us, and within us, too. Always, she was a gentle, adoring old lady who stroked my face and looked into my eyes as though she saw her entire world renewed somewhere in their depth. To sit in her lap on a chair by the window, to have my head patted until every hair was in place, and to feel her hand run lovingly down my arm—these were among the blessings of my early years.

It was Bubbeh's unalloyed pleasure to comb my hair each morning, and my unalloyed pleasure to watch us both in the mirror as its tousled disarray took shape under a touch so tender that it felt like an anointing. She would position my head under the faucet, running water at exactly the right temperature and then toweling me just enough to tame the confused flurry of moist strands that resulted. The hair was then combed forward until it lay plastered and flat against my head, and ready for the part that was formed by running the tip of the hard rubber comb back to front on the left. Having done that, she would comb both sides straight back from the wide forehead that declared me to be my mother's child. And then came the ultimate moment, when the *chubikle*—called a pompadour by those who, unlike Bubbeh and me, could not speak Yiddish—was skillfully shaped. Standing at my left, she would lightly place the flat of her hand about two inches behind the leading edge of my wet and pliant hair, press firmly down and forward along the length of her index finger, and there it was—a high, soft wave that always made me smile with pleasure when it appeared.

I continued to leave the molding of the *chubikle* to her until my mother died the week following my eleventh birthday. Then I took responsibility for it. It would not be until I had completed my surgical training and gotten married that I stopped pressing Bubbeh's *chubikle* into my wet hair each morning and after every shower.

Other than Bubbeh, the adults in my family spoke English with varying degrees of proficiency—Rose the best, my father by far the worst. Harvey and I usually communicated with them in the native tongue of America, although each of us was likely to insert an occasional Yiddish word or term into our speech.

My father had arrived alone from Bessarabia in 1907, during his late teen years, but youth did not stand in the way of his heroically managing to resist any significant degree of assimilation. His immunity to the surrounding culture and his avoidance of available aids such as the ubiquitous immigrant night schools of the time has been a never-ending source of bafflement to me, and I sometimes used to wonder whether such an extraordinary feat required a conscious act of will.

I wondered about something else, too, and I will probably always wonder about it. Daddy never spoke of the family he left behind in the Bessarabian town of Novoselitz, nor would he tell us why he did not write to them or they to him. Over the years, I was able to patch together only small bits and pieces of their family history.

The family name means "needle man" (the Yiddish word is pronounced *nuddleman*), or tailor, and like many other European Jewish surnames, it derived from the occupation of a forebear. Meyer's grandfather came from a family of five sons, all but one of whom abandoned their original name of Weinberg. My Weinberg great-grandfather had chosen to rename himself Nuddleman as part of a strategy aimed at avoiding conscription into the Russian army, where Jews faced a mandatory thirty-year period of service without promotion. An exception was made if a family had only one son, who would be permitted to stay at home to help with whatever small enterprise they were engaged in. Nuddleman was the name my father brought with him to the immigration station at Castle Garden when he arrived there alone and virtually penniless. The spelling I inherited was probably the product of an official's attempt to put English letters to Meyer's pronunciation, or it may have made its appearance with the arrival of the two uncles who had preceded him.

What the Weinberg boys did in order to escape the hardship of enforced military servitude was hardly an original scheme. Four of them having changed their names, each claimed to be an only son. The authorities must have winked—perhaps having been bribed to do so—at this sort of very obvious dissembling, because it was so commonly utilized by desperate young men during the middle and late nineteenth century. To the traditional Jews of Eastern Europe, surnames were of little consequence, being used only for legal or other official purposes. At the time young Weinberg transformed himself into young Nuddleman, it had been less than a century since governments began to insist that all citizens have a surname. To Jews, surnames continued to be of far less importance than patronymics—for example, Yitzchak ben Avraham (Isaac, son of Abraham), or Rivkah bas Yaacov (Rebecca, daughter of Jacob). In such an atmosphere, men and women forsook their family names without pangs of conscience, because their heritage dwelled in other things. In time, I would do the same.

I learned all this Nudelman lore from a few conversations with distant cousins, but I did have just a bit of more personal information. I came by it in later years, through my interpretation of two old photographs among the many more recent ones displayed under the plate-glass top of the bureau in my parents' bedroom. I have not seen either of those pictures in almost forty-five years, but I remember both as though they were lying before me at this moment.

One was of Daddy's entire family, minus him. It was no different from the hundreds of similar portraits I had seen of families in those times and places, except for the appearance of the three teenage boys standing solemnly alongside their older sister, behind their seated middle-aged parents. In the photo, my grandmother Minge and my bearded grandfather Noach stare without expression into the camera, looking exactly like the old-world Jewish elders that they are. Their plain, slightly plumpish dark-eyed daughter (whose name I never learned) stands to the right, behind her seated father. Alongside are her three younger brothers, who look remarkably like Russian peasant boys. Their short hair, about the length of a crew cut, is light in color and could in fact be blond. Were it not for the company with whom they are seen, there is nothing that might suggest to an observer that they are Jewish.

The other photo was of a staunchly erect young man wearing the belted and strapped parade uniform of a private in the Russian army. His left hand grips a cane, upon which he depends for support, and his leg on that side is held stiffly in front of him, as though he cannot bend it at the knee. The proud soldier's hair is darker than it was in the other photo, and he is strikingly handsome. This is one of the sons shown in the other picture—whose name I never learned—now grown to manhood and recovering from wounds sustained in the Great War. I am guessing this last, because it was not something that Daddy told me. He never spoke of any of the people in these two photos, any more than he did of the circumstances of his leaving them. It was tacitly understood that no one would ask him about these things. I was a teenager before I heard the least word of the people in the photograph, and even then only because of the events of World War II. I did not learn any of the young people's names until one of the four, my uncle Avram, somehow traced our address and wrote—in Yiddish, of course—from his home in Buenos Aires, hoping to reestablish contact with the brother he had not seen or heard from in almost half a century. My father did not answer those letters. I never asked if Avram was the young soldier.

Although estranged from his immediate family, Daddy nevertheless found a home with one of his father's brothers upon arriving in America. That uncle had four small children, one of whom,

Willie, was destined to play a large and devoted role in Daddy's life and in mine. There was also a close relationship with another uncle who lived in that overcrowded warren of tenements, pushcarts, and disease that has become miraculously transformed into a place of nostalgia by a generation that never knew its privations—the Lower East Side of New York City.

I have little idea of how my father sustained himself in his first American years, beyond his telling me that he managed to scrape together enough money to buy a candy store and then went broke with it.

"I was a lousy businessman," he would tell me in Yiddish. "Altogether too easy a mark. Here's the kind of thing that used to happen. A woman would come in and ask for a glass of cherry soda, which I would mix up for her. She'd drink more than half of it and then complain, saying, 'You made it too sweet, Meyer,' so I'd fill the glass again with seltzer from the fountain. She'd take another long drink and say, 'You ruined it, Meyer. Now there's no cherry taste anymore.' So I'd squirt in more syrup. Of course, then she'd whine that it was too sweet again, but not till she'd taken another big swig. Again, I'd put in more seltzer. And that's how it went: 'Meyer this and Meyer that, and more syrup and more seltzer, and more seltzer and more syrup, and who knows what else, Meyer'— until Meyer finally lost his shirt from these kinds of things. To tell you the truth, Sheppy, I was just as happy, because I hated dragging those big blocks of ice from the curb into the store at five o'clock every morning."

After a few other failures in small business, Daddy, like so many other Jewish immigrants of the time, finally sought out a job working at a sewing machine in one of the garment industry sweatshops along Seventh Avenue. Over the years, he would be employed in a series of such places, always as an "operator," which meant that he and the others so designated sewed together dresses whose parts had been cut and fashioned by more skilled craftspeople. Each of the shops was ruled over by the Boss, a man considered the natural enemy of the employees and of the International Ladies' Garment Workers' Union, founded to confront him in every possible arena from wages to ventilation. Caricatured in the ILGWU literature and strike posters as demanding, avaricious, and caring not a whit for the welfare of the mostly Jewish and Italian immigrants who toiled in his shop, he fought each improvement that cut into his profits. Every one of the bosses I was ever told about seemed to fit the mold, at least as described by those who labored for him.

In a sense, Daddy had entered the family occupation. One of his uncles, Shoil Nudelman, had done the same, and found himself working next to a pretty blue-eyed blonde from Novaradugk, named Vitsche Lutsky. Shoil was the matchmaker, and the two young people, both in their late twenties, married in 1919. My parents' relationship was one of incomprehensible complexity and inconsistency, and even now I struggle to understand it.

I have no idea whether my parents had a romantic courtship, because I never heard them speak of it in later years, except one day when, at the age of nine, I asked my mother how Daddy had proposed. She smiled shyly in his direction and reminded him that he had done it by saying, "Will you go away with me?" The recollection of it brought a look of sweet gentleness into his eyes, but the moment lasted only a second, as though such warm memories were not to be permitted to intrude on the practical events of life's current realities. In later years, I would learn from relatives that the decision of Meyer and Vitsche to marry soon became the cause of a strong undercurrent of resentment in Momma's family. I never definitively ascertained the source of it, but it was hinted that it arose from Rose's continuing single status, because old-world conventions dictated that she should have married first.

So many families of that time had a maiden aunt living with them that she has become a familiar figure in fiction and memoir, and I presume to put Tante Aya among them. From my earliest recollection of her, she seemed interminably busy. She bustled her chunky little self off each morning to the 183rd Street subway station, took the train to her job in a dressmaking loft in New York's Garment District, and then trudged home each evening just before supper. Rose was part of a small circle of unmarried women friends who went together to the movies, to the Yiddish theater, and occasionally to the Metropolitan Opera. One of them always took us kids to the circus when it made its annual visit to Madison Square Garden.

There was a certain brisk and businesslike femininity about Tante Aya. The years had brought added pounds to a figure that was revealed in the old photos as alluringly curvaceous. She was said to have once been very attractive, when her head of thick, buoyant hair was still blond and her light blue eyes flashed with the fire of spirited youth and a razor-sharp wit. Relatives told tales of rejected suitors and her haughty ways with those who continued to pursue in vain. She was a constant presence in our lives—generous and greathearted and at the same time just a bit tart-tongued and minimally tolerant of childish misbehavior. Tante Aya had the energy of a small, squat dynamo. I would never learn the entire secret of the contempt that she and Bubbeh exuded toward my father, or of the obvious ill will for them that he seemed to go out of his way to demonstrate in return.

Rose had had no shortage of shtetl-bred suitors. No matter how faded the photographs of those days, it is obvious that—even measured against her three attractive sisters—she had a remarkably lovely face. Her hair was just a bit blonder and thicker than theirs, her eyes a slightly lighter blue. Without doubt, she was the beauty of the family. But there was a haughty selectiveness in the way she repeatedly rejected the inelegant swains who pursued her. She seemed, I was told by people who knew her in that youthful time, to be figuratively (and sometimes literally, too, I suppose) keeping them at arm's length, letting them know that she was made for better men than they. I am certain that it is not my imagination that detects the merest trace of a pout of independence on the lips of the aloof young woman in the old photographs, nor is it my admiration for her absolute self-sufficiency of later years that convinces me that it can be seen in her eyes even at that early time. She was like her mother in this, undaunted by the buffeting of an oafish world, and intolerant of imperfection in herself or others. Not only did those two proud women not suffer fools gladly; their contempt was overtly made evident to any boor who, in their supercritical estimation, earned it.

The young Meyer Nudelman was hardly a boor, but neither was he a very polished specimen of a rising young immigrant. The problem, as it was described to me decades later, was that Meyer seemed unwilling or perhaps unable to do what was required to improve his station. It seemed to the Lutsky women beyond understanding that a man should fail to make any attempt to better himself. To his bride's family, Meyer was still a greenhorn. But there could have been no complaints about the way Meyer looked. In those days, he was a slim, sturdily built man, whose eyes seemed never to lose that appearance of deep sensitivity with which he viewed the world until the day he died.

In his youth, Meyer Nudelman looked like a proud man, and he was. The inconsistency between that and his inertia in attempting to better himself will always puzzle me. His hair, almost black, was parted on the left and combed toward the side, but it had a way of curling itself into a small Napoleonic wave that fell forward onto his broad, high forehead. Even after it began its lateral spread in later years, that well-nostriled Jewish nose of his conveyed an image of certitude and strength, especially as it overlooked a determined, finely lipped mouth and a strong chin. Meyer's appearance as a young man gave the impression of self-confidence. Even on his limited budget, he made certain that his clothes fit him perfectly, and he took meticulous care of them. But he was a man who stood alone, and at a distance.

His distance was apparent in all things, even in the way he spoke—especially in the language of this country, in which he never found his way. Many of the words and expressions and pronunciations that peppered his speech were inimitable. They were his alone. The next-door neighbor was "ah naybrid ti me"; the dish served at the end of a meal was "rezoyve." When coming in from a game of stickball, I might be told to "Vosh you doidy fayste"; should I delay, it would be said "dvized," or twice. "Tschikahgy" was a midwestern metropolis, as was "Tsintsineddy," whereas "Sen Frensooskie" looked out on the Pacific Ocean. My father knew about these places, although he neglected to become a "tsititsnerr" of the United States until he had been living here for almost forty years.

Though Daddy never said a word about anything he had left behind in Novoselitz, Momma's family did just the opposite about the environs of their town of origin. As we listened to Momma, Bubbeh, and Rose speak, it sometimes seemed that the golden land was the far-off one that had been left, and not this one to which they had come. Their tales of sweet remembrance about that treasured place nostalgically recalled as *der heym*—"our home"— in Russia were many. Its distant rhythms seemed far less turbulent than those of this thief America, or *America gonef,* as they so often called their new place of residence, because it had robbed them of so much.

But there was also an underlying theme that sooner or later would emerge when stories of *der heym* were being told, and it was a far less peaceful one than the thread running through the narratives of family and holidays and synagogue. These darker bits were of the hatred of Jews by the peasants of Novaradugk and every other city and shtetl of the Pale. For them, Bubbeh harbored hatred in return, and scorn for their coarse, illiterate ways. And in the matter of goyim—Gentiles—Bubbeh's teachings were far from unspoken. To her, *a goy blaybt a goy* ("a Gentile will always remain a Gentile"), even here in America, where she perceived the Christians around her to be blood brothers of—or at least stand-ins for— those she had known long ago. She had packed the memories of their enmity into the trunkful of possessions that she brought with her from Novaradugk. She would be sure that her grandchildren knew about such things.

To Bubbeh, every goy was a potential danger, ready at any time to steal from a Jew's small store of goods or even take part in a pogrom. How many stories did I hear of Ivan, the generic Russian peasant? He was brutish and big; uneducated and provoked to commit obscene acts because of his fear of the Jew's culture; Godless and yet intent on avenging the murder of his God. In America, Bubbeh let us know in not-subtle ways, his name was John, and he was often Irish or Italian. But just beyond his genial tipping of the hat and Sunday-morning righteousness, he was the same drunken goy as always and everywhere, who resented the sight of us.

In fact, there were reasons to believe Bubbeh's tales of hatred against us; I had my own experience of such things. I saw Ivan— or John—in action a few times in that East Bronx neighborhood where we lived until I was almost four. One episode remains so vivid that it plays like a motion picture on the screen of my memory.

On the afternoon of the first day of Rosh Hashanah, the New Year, it is customary for observant Jews to go to the banks of a body of flowing water and cast their sins into it, in the symbolic form of bits of bread. The year I was three, Daddy let me join the family and perhaps thirty other members of our congregation on this pilgrimage to the edge of a nearby stream called Pugsley's Creek. To get there, our line of marchers had to pass through a neighborhood of small homes lining one side of a block inhabited mostly by the families of blue-collar immigrants from Poland and

Germany. A vacant lot of rubble and wild grass occupied the opposite side of the street. The first day of the holiday having been on the Sabbath, the service, called Tashlich, was taking place on a warm, sunny Sunday afternoon.

The adults carried prayer books under their arms. With us children herded closely within the group's ranks, we moved warily, as though in a hushed parade, through the short block of what was known to be hostile territory. My father looked dignified in his only hat, cleaned and blocked for the holiday—a practice he would follow until the end of his life. Some of the boys wore yarmulkes. The heads of the older women were covered by black kerchiefs of the sort Bubbeh always wore. We kids had been warned not to make any commotion, and even the youngest of us knew why. It seemed to me as though every florid-faced factory worker, every heavy-bellied housewife, every towheaded devil-child with a crew cut was sitting in anticipation of our arrival, lounging on the paint-chipped front steps and porches of those ten or twelve little wooden houses lining the street on our left. These people looked nothing like us. The only thing we had in common with them was the warm September sun, and our mutual contempt.

The sneering, scornful goyim glared with threatening eyes as we went by, and shouted out their stored-up hatred as though they had been waiting there since Golgotha. They hooted at us, bellowing those timeless obscenities with which Jews have long been familiar, passed on through generations of thick-necked bullies to whom the mere sight of us has been an incitement to violence. "Dirty Jews, kikes, goddamn sheenies." Those large sweating men and their harridan women screamed the words I already knew, and worse imprecations, which I did not understand. Some of them shook their fists at us and loudly incited a few of their gleeful, overexcited offspring to run alongside our line of march, taunting us with foul words and making threatening gestures with their waving arms. Just as we passed the last house, a few of the mean-looking dogs that had been straining against the grip of their plethoric masters were all at once let loose on us. I remember the animals as ungroomed and dirty; unlike our bulky human tormentors, all of the four-footed curs seemed to have been small. Their yelping and snarls augmented the yelping and snarls of their two-legged fellows, who kept screaming in hectoring volleys.

Walking purposefully at the head of his intimidated band, our heavily bearded little leader would not gratify the barbarians by hurrying his pace, but I had no idea that this was meant to be the rabbi's dignified response to indignity. As much as they might have taken a dim view of his show of proud determination, our adults must have known why he was acting in what certainly was to them an unnecessarily provocative manner. But to a frightened little boy with no notion of defiance, it seemed senseless not to flee. Caught between rabbi and rabble, there was no choice but to continue to absorb the menace being flung at us. No matter how tightly my father gripped my hand, I knew only that I was scared and trembling. I wanted to run. Daddy—he of the terrible temper—was subdued and, like all of the other grown-ups and the older children, held his eyes fixed on the back of the person just in front of him. Whether from wisdom or timidity, no one was about to look directly at any face in the jeering mob, lest the eye contact goad an enraged goy to excess more physical than what had already been flung at our somber procession. These malevolent beings seemed barely able to restrain themselves from such violence. I could not look to Daddy for protection, and I felt ashamed of his helplessness—of the helplessness of all the adults. I was a little boy even ashamed of himself.

The loutish goyim had power and we had trembling; they were dangerous and strong and we were cowardly and weak; they were the threat and we were the threatened. In every way, they were overwhelming in their derision and loathing. That we had contempt for them and for the hateful religion in whose name they committed such outrages only worsened our humiliation.

These were the brutes my Bubbeh always spoke of, who had terrorized and even murdered Jews in *der heym*. In that faraway place of her unfading memories, they had mocked the mockies and slaughtered the sheenies. We were, after all, Christ-killers. The goy was always the enemy, even here in America.

III

The year is still 1934. It is spring, the hour is suppertime, and we are gathered around three sides of a rectangular kitchen table. The long fourth side is pressed up against the wall, because the room is not big enough to allow a complete surround of chairs. We are eating boiled fish, so it must be Monday or Thursday, because those are always the fish days. My father sits remote and expressionless, as he predictably does during meals. He is at the end of the table farthest from the stove, looking only at his food, as though no one else is near him. I am at his left, and my mother is alongside of me. Next to her is Harvey and then my aunt Rose, our four wooden chairs pressed together. The stove only a few feet behind her, Bubbeh sits at the opposite end of the table from my father, dressed as always in a floor-length black skirt and a white blouse covered in large navy blue polka dots. The ever-present black kerchief, her *facheylke,* covers all but a narrow frontal rim of her graying brown hair, which is parted in the middle. I am only three, but I have long since known that Daddy never speaks to either Bubbeh or Aunt Rose. Neither does he ever so much as look at them if it can be avoided. The animosity between them is so great that I have seen him slam a cabinet door when Bubbeh happens to enter the kitchen while he is there. We are eating in silence—silence, that is, except for Daddy's loud chomping.

The fish is filled with bones, but not the portion that has been carefully prepared for the youngest person at the table. Momma has meticulously dissected that small mound of pristine white bits of flesh until it is free of anything that might possibly injure my palate. Even seven-year-old Harvey's portion has not received the same thorough attention.

In the next image, the meal is not quite over, but Daddy has already pushed back his chair and left the table without a word, impatient to be away from his wife's mother and sister. He is sitting in the living room, reading the *Jewish Daily Forward*. A large piece of uneaten food still remains on his plate, and it looks very different from the soft, delicate flesh that I have just finished wolfing down. Daddy's is a section cut from the fish's middle, and something about it virtually proclaims that this dangerous bone-filled thing is what my father eats. The very danger of the fish and the very danger of taking it make my next action inevitable.

Momma's head is turned away from me for a moment, because a quiet conversation has begun at the table now that my father is in the living room; she is saying something to her mother and sister. Quickly, I thrust my arm toward Daddy's large plate, pull free a handful of bony fish, and gulp it down before anyone notices.

A piercing burst of sharp, lacerating pain from somewhere deep in the left side of my throat shrieks at me that I have made a terrible mistake. I have taken what is my father's, and retribution will swiftly follow. I let out a high-pitched screeching sound and am immediately surrounded by adults, who know at once what I have done. My father is suddenly there, and anxious Bubbeh and Aunt Rose step quickly backward and away from me, until they have pushed themselves against the stove behind them, in order to be out of his way. Ignoring my distraught mother, he stands over me and shouts at my unforgivable indiscretion. More than sixty-five years later, it is impossible today for me to remember his words, even had I comprehended them, but I know the gist of what he would have said in that odd, infuriated semi-English of his own invention.

"Khazerl du, vod kind khutspa you got vod you takink mine piece sopper? You, vod you tink you sotch a gantser mentsh all ahf ah sotten?" ("You little pig! What kind of gall do you have that you would take a piece of my supper? You think you're such a big man all of a sudden?")

In the hubbub of voices, there is immediately talk of Dr. Daly, who is holding regular evening hours at his office in the small brick building almost across the street from our house. The mere mention of such a fearsome place makes me tremble even more. That den of torment is, after all, the chamber of needles and of flat wooden sticks being rammed into my protesting mouth. The confusion of voices—Daddy speaking only to Momma, she trying to reply to both sides—only magnifies the fright. They are saying that I have a bone stuck in my throat, that it will have to be pulled out, that "No, Sheppy, it won't hurt at all." I will not be comforted, though my father's outburst has by now petered away and he begins trying to speak reassuringly to me, even stroking one of my heaving shoulders in that clumsy way of his, which just makes everything worse. He looks sad for me, and worried. His expression and the bit of gleaming moisture in his eyes make him at this moment appear on the verge of tears. Daddy's anger abated, he wants to take me in his arms, but I will have none of it.

Though I do not (or can no longer, for the pain) speak, I am shaking my head adamantly: I will not be dragged off to Dr. Daly. It is then suggested that I be taken for a walk in the evening air, allegedly to make me feel better. Since I remain resistant to my father's overtures of comforting and my mother is too upset for it, Tante Aya will accompany me. I suspect nothing.

In my next recalled image, Tante Aya and I are at the stoop in front of Dr. Daly's building. Trustingly, I allow myself to be taken inside. Several pairs of hands must have seized me as soon as I crossed the threshold of the building, because I next see myself being held down in something like a dentist's chair, feet flailing against the legs of Tante Aya and a woman dressed in white, and trying ineffectually to croak out something like outrage and protest. The glistening pate of Dr. Daly is hovering over me. In his right hand, he holds what looks like a small pair of silver pliers. Just as my mouth flings itself wide open in an attempt at a loud scream of defense against what I know he plans to do, he plunges the instrument of torture down my throat. In a moment, the diabolically grinning prince of darkness and vaccinations is holding the evil tool up in the air, an unbelievably long sliver of white fishbone clamped tightly in its jaws. As soon as I am let go, I stop struggling, as though a switch had been turned off. A few minutes later, I am in Mr. Sweer's drugstore with Tante Aya, spooning up chocolate and vanilla ice cream from a Dixie cup.

It is late at night, and the entire family has long been asleep. I am awakened by the insistent banging of someone's fist on the door to the apartment, and an angry male voice shouting muffled and unintelligible words that sound threatening. From my bed in the room I share with Bubbeh and Tante Aya, I can just make out my mother in her nightdress, standing alone in the hallway, about five feet from the door. As my eyes accustom themselves to the darkness, I see that she appears to be waiting and hesitant, as though not sure what to do. My father is not there. Bubbeh and Tante Aya are motionless in bed, and I wonder why. Perhaps they do not hear the commotion, but how can that be, when the noise and my thoughts are so tumultuous?

I get up and run toward the hallway, because at the age of four it is safer to be close to Momma than to remain in bed, by myself and unprotected. But even when I am standing there with my arms wrapped tightly around her knees, how can I know that this raging beast—though I am still befuddled by sleep, I have by now become convinced that he is, in fact, drunk—will not be able to get at us? Even though I do not understand everything he says, as his voice is muffled and slurred by rage, and the door's thickness of metal separates us, I am sure that it is Momma he is after.

The man is wild and out of control, and he is calling my mommy bad names that I cannot quite make out. No matter the baffling through which his insistent clamor reaches us, there is no question of how he is speaking to her. She had better open up, he thunders in a rumbling crescendo of threat. And then he adds something ominous, which sounds like "if you know what's good for you!"

Momma answers firmly that she will not let him in, and there is no hint in her voice of any fear like the fear I am feeling. The unyielding stiffness of her legs tells me that she is apprehensive. But she is also adamant. The man's rage mounts, and the door seems every second less of a barrier to the invasion of our uncertain stronghold. Suddenly, he hurls his final terrible warning: "I'm taking my strap off." As garbled as it is, the sound of those words from its unrecognizable source thunders through the dense metal as if he were already standing belt in hand before us, ready to do with Momma whatever it is he wants. The "whatever it is," I know, is something only a man has the power to accomplish. He will beat her with the weapon whipped from around his waist.

Momma seems to waiver and be unsure for a moment, but nothing changes in her response. If she is not frightened into submission by the dangerous closeness of that warning, I will know that she can take care of everything about this awful moment. And he, the storming madman, is the everything. She raises her voice now to be sure that he can hear each of the two words she is about to say as a final dismissal: "GO AVAY!"

There is no further sound from the other side of the door. Momma picks me up, strokes the side of my head, and whispers the familiar reassurance that has so often calmed me at difficult times. Though I have not been crying, she says, *"Sha, shtil, kindele. Zolst gut shlofn"* ("Hush, my little one, and sleep well"). She puts me into bed, pulls up the covers, and kisses my forehead.

I never heard my parents speak about that night; I never found out where my father was. Those unnerving events might just as well not have happened. But they did.

Psychologists tell us that we repress hurtful memories and hold on to the good. And yet these fearful moments and the emotions they evoked are the ones that always present themselves in the images passing before my eyes whenever I recall those early years in the East Bronx. But all was not fear and danger. Far from it, for at the same time I was a child imbued with a sense of his envelopment within a nurturing protectiveness, and by this I do not mean only my mother's. I lived in a fragile cocoon, but it was a cocoon nevertheless.

To Bubbeh, to Aunt Rose, and even to my father, we three children—Harvey and I and our cousin, Arline—represented, I came to realize much later, their only triumph over the series of hardships that emigration to the United States had inflicted on them. Illness, death, financial struggle—these had been the accompaniments of their American journey. The three of us were the emotional wherewithal that enabled them to persist in the face of the misfortune and even the tragedy that had befallen them since leaving Russia three decades earlier. I would, in time, come to understand that we were their consolation for all that the unkept promise of America had taken away from them; we were their reward for persevering; we were their proof that from all the heartbreak a portion of human redemption had nevertheless been snatched. We were their hope.

From my earliest perception, Daddy seemed the one person in my small orbit who stood at somewhat of a remove from me, who did not quite know how to approach me or touch me without there being something ungainly about it. His hands could not hold a small boy effortlessly, and his attempts at a gentleness of touch were awkward. He would try to express his affection by stroking my cheek, but the inadvertent clumsiness of the gesture would make me pull back in a sudden defensive movement, and he would become offended and angry. These were the times when his eyes lost the appearance of looking outward from some place of sensitivity deep within him. At such moments, his glance hardened with his temper. I had to be wary of these sudden changes. It was not the fury itself, though, but its unpredictability that made the volatile outbursts so frightening to me. The entire household was in thrall to them, never knowing when its quiet order might be shattered by the consequences of some infraction, imagined or real. When I was somewhat older, I saw that things did not always turn out the way he wished. He would reach for something and knock it over, attempt to take a step forward and have to be sure that he was planting his foot just the way he wanted to. His life seemed full of small failures and perceived slights. In spite of every one of his inherent disabilities, though, I somehow knew, with that unerring sense that growing children have, that he loved me, that he obviously cared deeply about me. But his expressions of it were strange, and they made me feel strange, too.

Into this atmosphere of unstable serenity—into the fragile cocoon—there one day intruded a frightening series of events. Although not uncommon at that time, such a situation is fortunately extremely unlikely to occur today. Now, retrieving the old memory, the sequence of images and brief bits of rolling film are easily brought forward, as though into the present. With them come the feelings.

It is a brisk morning in the late autumn of 1934, and I am

almost four years old. My mother and I have just left the corner grocery, and she is deeply engrossed in Yiddish conversation with a neighbor, who has brought along her son, a bit older than I. A few feet away on the sidewalk just outside the store stand two large upright blocks of ice waiting to be taken indoors for the day's refrigeration of tubs of butter, cheese, and the steel pails of milk and cream from which every customer's order will be ladled into bottles and jars. As the conversation wears on and on, we two bored boys squat alongside the frozen hexahedrons and begin to run our eager tongues over their deliciously cold edges. When notice is finally taken of our little mischief, the prolonged chat abruptly ends, and our stolen moments of clandestine pleasure end with it.

In a day or so, I feel the beginnings of a sore throat. I am sicker and a bit feverish on the following morning, then worsen as the day wears on. It is becoming difficult to breathe. Dr. Daly appears at my bedside, taps my chest, and listens for whatever he listens for with that peculiar snakelike instrument stuck into his ears. He takes Momma into the living room, and I know they are talking about me. Perhaps he is telling her the disturbing news that an epidemic of diphtheria has broken out in the city this week and that several children are already dead.

That evening, Dr. Daly returns and hears the rasping sound I make with each labored inhalation.

Suddenly, our flat is filled with blue-uniformed men too large for its cramped space. I am hurriedly examined by a doctor dressed all in white, who seems not to pay attention to my softly weeping mother, or even to my father. They seem confused and uncertain. The unfamiliar hands of the burly invaders pick me up from my cot. I am put on a stretcher and immediately swaddled tightly in a confining blanket, with restraining straps to prevent my hysterical attempts to break loose.

I am taken on the stretcher down the front steps of the house and out the entrance, then carried through a small crowd of curious neighbors assembled near the wide-open doors of a city ambulance backed up against the curb. Lying there immobilized and being jostled and bounced, I find myself staring directly into the light of an adjacent streetlamp. I try to lift my head to see into the boxlike conveyance waiting for me, all the more threatening because of the blinding glare of artificial light surrounding it. The stretcher is guided through the doors and they are slammed shut, leaving me alone inside with the white-suited doctor and one of the blue-coated men. Everyone I know has been left behind.

When the next image flashes into my mind, I am sitting upright on the edge of a white enameled table, its hard metal surface softened only by a little thin mattress covered in a sheet. A woman wearing a white dress and an oddly shaped white hat—like Dr. Daly's helper—is holding me steady by the shoulders and speaking softly into my ear, but I am too frightened to understand her. The walls are white; the ceiling is white—everything is white. Several big-bellied men in white stand alongside the table, looking at me and talking to one another. I know it is about me. The doctor who brought me here is not among them.

I try to call out for my mother, but that word—*Mommy*—never comes out and I can feel myself choking with the attempt. After this, I remember nothing until I awaken early the next morning in an open ward full of children. There is a large pane of thick clear glass behind my bed, and beyond it a window through which I can see sailboats on a body of water.

(Many years later, I had learned enough about medicine and the epidemics of diphtheria in those days to know the subsequent events that would have taken place that night in an examining room adjacent to the pediatric ward. Diphtheria progresses rapidly, and my throat was by then almost completely closed off by the shaggy gray thickness of the circumferential membrane of strangling infection that the disease lays down on the inner lining of a struggling child's windpipe. Once in the hospital, strong hands would have held me immobile while a metallic retractor was forced between my clenched teeth in order to keep my mouth wide open. Since any attempt at anesthesia in such an advanced situation was extremely hazardous in those days, one of the doctors would have rammed a surgical clamp or similar instrument down my throat while the others, probably orderlies, held my head and body tightly to keep me from jerking away from him. The instrument would then have been forced into the plane between the obstructing membrane and the inner lining of my windpipe, to which it so densely adhered. With utmost speed, the clamp would have been swept back and forth a few times to separate the two layers as much as possible. By creating a space between the raw, bloody surfaces, the infected pathological tissue would have been sufficiently loosened to enable the gruesome process to reach its climax, when the shaggy gray plug of asphyxiation and death was torn free and pulled up and out through my mouth. I can only imagine the medical team's relief when the therapeutic savagery had been completed and I took my first long, gurgly breath. The instant improvement in my bluish skin color would have told them that they had succeeded.)

My parents are still not with me. I see one of those women in white and I yell at the top of my recovered voice, even though it will be days before I can speak without a raw discomfort in my throat. "I want my mommy!" I cry. It does no good, so I repeat it, this time louder. It still does no good.

The nurses try kindness, but to no avail. I will not stop calling for my mother, always with the same brief formula of words: "I want my mommy! I want my mommy!"

The ward is a large square space. The head of each of its perhaps thirty beds is positioned a few feet from one of three walls, leaving a wide central area where nurses and orderlies scurry about. The fourth wall contains the entranceway, with desks and some cabinets for bedding and instruments on each side of it. I am the first child on the right as the ward is entered.

My bed and the two next to it are each enclosed on three sides by huge floor-to-ceiling plates of glass, the foot end being open to the busy center of the ward. (The three glass enclosures held the patients deemed to be the sickest and most contagious. I had been taken to the Willard Parker Hospital, the city's central facility for the treatment of patients with infectious disease, located at the lowermost tip of Manhattan. It was a long el and subway ride from the East Bronx.)

Late on the first day, my mother and father appear. I try to talk to them through the glass at the head of the bed, behind which they are standing. But it acts as a baffle and they seem very far away. I reach out to touch them and they each do the same, but we cannot. We touch only our own sides of the glass. I beg them to take me home, and we are all crying. I have never before seen tears in my father's eyes.

They come again the next day and every day after that, but they never take me home. All three of us are strangers here; nobody has a Yiddish, an Italian, or even an Irish accent. Why don't they sound like the people I know? Among them, Momma and Daddy are curiosities, as though they have just arrived from another continent. Standing there, separated from me by the glass, they seem diminished, and lost. It adds to my desolation. The only thing they can do for me is to take me home, and even that they cannot do— or will not. And then one day, my father does come to take me home. Momma is not with him, but I know that I will see her soon.

I am wrapped up snugly in a plaid blanket and my father is holding me in his arms at the head of a wide flight of stairs leading to the lobby. He will carry me down those steps and we will get into a taxi, though we cannot really afford it.

As I recall this scene today, its inevitably accompanying feeling comes rushing back, as inseparable as if it were a part of the picture, like my father or me or the blanket: I am unsure whether Daddy has the strength and the steadiness to carry me down that long staircase. My perception of his weakness had already begun.

For my parents, the terrifying experience of seeing me struggle to breathe was a stark reliving of a still-raw anguish. Eight years earlier, their firstborn child, also a boy of three, had suddenly been taken from them by a progression of events frighteningly like the one they were witnessing on that awful night when I was rushed to the hospital. Maishele was recovering from a seemingly straightforward case of measles when he developed an unanticipated bronchial pneumonia, which was an occasional complication of that childhood disease. After two days of their physician's desperate attempts to save him, he died in gasping agony of air hunger and infection.

Bubbeh, Tante Aya, and my parents were devastated, but Maishele's tragic death took a particularly great toll on my father. Throughout my childhood, Bubbeh would tell me story after story of Maishele's precocious speech, his clever doings, his sunny disposition. In him were invested all the American hopes of his family. He was the center of my father's universe and the focus of his love. The money difficulties, the oppressive gloom of years lost in a personal inertia, the strain of living with Bubbeh and Tante Aya—all of these were tolerable because each evening my father could return home to his adored little boy. When Maishele died, something of Daddy went into the grave with him. By every account I would hear in later years, my father was never the same man after the pervasive pall of his son's death descended on him. Maishele's departure was the climactic stroke of misfortune, the ultimate signal to abandon whatever small pursuit of the American dream he had attempted. Even the birth of Harvey a year later could not compensate for the magnitude of his loss. This first—this special—child took a piece of my father's spirit with him, and whatever recovery Daddy might try to make from it could never be more than partial.

Unspoken by Daddy though it was, the burden of that unbearable loss would bend his back and assail his soul every day of the three long decades left of his life. He could not free himself of the lost hope of what might have been.

IV

My father's unsteadiness slowly increased as the years passed, and so did my awareness of it. By the time I was eight or nine, I had begun to devise ways of separating myself from him when the two of us went for walks outside of our immediate neighborhood. I did not want strangers to know that I was the son of a man so marked by disability.

Like so many immigrants of his generation—including all those in my family—Daddy never knew the date or year of his birth. But he must have been around forty when I was born. In the eyes of a young boy, he seemed older even than that. The stooped shoulders of a man who needed to be constantly attentive to the pavement in front of him, the extreme attention he paid to every anticipated step forward, and the intent look of concentration and worry that the effort brought to his careworn face—all of these made him appear many years beyond his age.

Before his difficulties became visible to others, and long after as well, Daddy loved to "tek ah vuk"—the longer the better—and I was his preferred companion on these rambling walks. Harvey's time and interest were taken up with his gang of friends, hours-long stickball games, and the sociability of candy stores. On the few occasions when he accompanied his father, he would become restless and make it known that he would rather be elsewhere. Blocks from home and enthusiastic to return to some game he had unwillingly left, he would sometimes rush off with barely a good-bye, abandoning Daddy, who would have to make his way back by himself.

I, on the other hand, was always available, and I enjoyed exploring other neighborhoods, no matter how many times we had traversed them on previous expeditions. When Daddy and I were outside the apartment, he seemed liberated. Something warm and good in him was set free when he escaped the presence of Bubbeh and Tante Aya, and this may have been the most important reason that he took so much pleasure in walking the long streets with me. During those times, he and I seemed just naturally to belong together. He never showed any anger then, and his enjoyment of our being with each other was evident. He became what he really was: a father who loved his son. And I was a son who felt happy to be with his father. In the apartment, on the other hand, Daddy was an outlander, estranged from everyone else. The soulfulness left his eyes at the least provocation, whether intended or not, and a look of smoldering discontent replaced it. When he resumed his at-home self, I would revert to the trepidation that his presence could instill in me. Once again, I would separate myself from him and cleave to the consistency of Momma, Bubbeh, and Tante Aya. So much of the joy I took in those walks came from being alone and far off with the man I wanted my father always to be.

"Tekkink ah vuk" with Daddy began when I was about four. During those early years, he would usually hold my hand in his, as fathers do with their small boys, but by the time I was six, it was no longer necessary. Being nine or ten when Daddy's unsteadiness had reached the point where I could no longer avoid recognizing it, I was old enough to know that others recognized it, too. If Daddy sometimes took my hand, it would be when he had to negotiate some irregular stretch of pavement, and he held it tightly.

The difficulties of walking were not the only ones that were gradually beginning to affect Daddy's movements. He seemed to need consciously to guide his spoon or fork from the plate to his lips, and the arc became at first hesitant and then after a few years decidedly erratic. Bits and drips of food would occasionally fall off a spoon and onto his lap or the table. The problem was worse when he had to contend with soup. After awhile, few of his ties or trousers were free of stains.

I was sure that Daddy was too preoccupied with his walking and his thoughts ever to have noticed how far I had begun to lag behind or the many yards I had run ahead, but how could he have been oblivious to it? I would rush up to him each time a particularly high or otherwise difficult sidewalk-to-gutter step needed to be negotiated and then would stay with him until we reached the other side of the street, my hand tightly intertwined in his. That alone should have given my game away, but neither of us spoke about it. I never let myself acknowledge until decades later that he must have known what I was doing during those years when his disabilities were first showing themselves so clearly and I was finding ways to deal with the emotion that I was ashamed to recognize as shame.

I took these walks not only alone with Daddy but sometimes with Momma, too. On evenings from late spring (usually not until Passover was done) until the High Holiday of Rosh Hashanah in September, the three of us would occasionally go for a long *shpatsir*, as we called it, after supper was over. Even without Harvey, it seemed like the one thing our little family could do together, free of the tensions within the walls of our apartment. Harvey was always elsewhere, off with his friends for one of those stickball games or congregating with them around the newsstand outside the corner candy store.

Our evening *shpatsir* took us long distances, miles in fact. Our direction was always northward across the busy boulevards that were among the main traffic arteries of the Bronx: Fordham Road, the Grand Concourse, upward along Jerome Avenue, or toward the large green expanse of St. James Park. When Momma walked between the two of us, Daddy's gait was so much more certain that I hardly noticed any of the strain in his steps—hardly. Holding Momma's left hand or strolling alongside her, I was distanced from the sight and some of the sound of him.

I paid little attention to the adults' conversation, which was conducted almost entirely in their disparately accented Yiddish—hers in the soft Litvak of the northern part of the Pale and his in the harsher near-Galitzianer of Bessarabia, in the south. It may be that the tones of Litvak are not, in fact, softer than Galitzianer; it may be that the soft belonged to Momma and the harsh to Daddy; it may be that I heard them as I believed them to be. Whatever the case, it was grown-up talk, and I had more interesting things on my mind. Besides, they spoke usually of troubles in the *mishpokhe*—the family—of one sort or another, and I hated to hear of more anguish than I had already been exposed to at home. There was always trouble to talk about, and never any solutions. If there were stories of triumph to be told during those walks, or of difficulties overcome, I never heard about them—or at least I don't remember them. Worry, pessimism, regret, discontent, anger—that was the agenda, and my parents seemed rarely to agree about any of it. As their accents differed, so did their viewpoints on matters great and small.

In fact, I hardly heard their discussions, and I rarely listened to the few sentences that penetrated my conscious mind. Trouble seemed something for my parents to think about, not me. For me, being within the vibrant bustle and the expectant air of the crowded Bronx avenues on those balmy evenings was like a promise of far-off places and later times, when I would be free of the cares of my family, and free of them as individuals, too—all of them. I loved them and I needed them, and I was already aware that they needed me, too. But they stood in my way. I felt only a child's naïve expectation of great things sure to come, and an enthusiasm for everything in that wider universe that I was trying to see.

I was six and seven and eight and nine—I saw no inconsistency between my need of my family and my need to be free of them. Surveying the exhilarating stimulation and even happiness that I was convinced the surrounding world held—and held in store for me—all I could think about on those walks was that I must be destined for escape. Like every other kid, I harbored a fantasy that I had not really been born into my family, and, like every other kid, I thought I was the only one who felt this kind of distance. I was among them but not of them. That certainty was never so clear as when I caught a glimpse of the rest of America as it could be seen all around me in the wide thoroughfares of the Bronx on those spring and summer evenings.

I loved the *shpatsirs* because it felt so natural for the three of us to be strolling together through the busy Bronx streets, surrounded by many others who were doing the same thing. The age of my parents and especially that of my father seemed less important at those times. Walking alongside Momma, I was a carefree little boy whose responsibility to his father's needs could be forgotten in the joy of just being a kid, watching the world take its pleasure around him.

The soles of my feet would invariably begin to ache near the end of a long *shpatsir,* when we were close to Fordham Road on the way home. But there was a remedy for it. Right next to the W. T. Grant department store, in the middle of the Fordham block between Morris and Walton Avenues, stood a commercial oasis the likes of which never lost its wonder for me. Behind a long white-topped counter opening directly onto the street, three or four pale-skinned teenagers dressed like a tourist's idea of Hawaiian natives were selling the fruit and juice of pineapples, oranges, and coconuts. The front of the counter was draped with the material of which grass skirts are made, and the wall behind was covered with a layer of crumpled green cellophane strands meant to look like tropical foliage. Spouts and spigots were everywhere, from which the young tribesmen drew juices and coconut milk. Portions of coconut meat and citrus fruit were displayed in wooden bowls and could be bought for nickels and dimes.

On each of our *shpatsirs,* I would begin complaining of sore feet when we came within a block or two of this ambrosian enterprise, and I would be bought a dime glass of one of its products in order to assuage me. A dime was a lot of money to my father, and knowing this made the sweet, ice-cold drink more tasty and even more therapeutic. I never gulped it; such a precious treat required savoring, and it had to be taken in small amounts to make it last as long as possible. The placebo always worked, very likely because I knew that my father could not really afford to throw his money around this way. Thus resuscitated, I would stop my grumbling and happily resume the walk home.

People changed dwelling places frequently in the New York City of those days, because landlords granted a discount on the rent, known as "two weeks concession." Half a month's rent was more money than the low rates charged by van companies, and it was thought to justify the upheaval of packing and unpacking, especially because the new apartment came with freshly painted walls and newly varnished floors. So often was the term used in adult conversation, I was certain that *concession* was a Yiddish word.

Perhaps the effects of President Roosevelt's economic reforms had brought a bit of unaccustomed prosperity to the poorly paid employees of the ladies' garment industry—and a note of equally unaccustomed hope into the family—but, for whatever reason, we had managed in late 1934 to leave Olmstead Avenue for a neighborhood that was a short but definite step upward. By the criteria of the time, 2314 Morris Avenue was even dignified by being referred to as an apartment house rather than as a tenement, but to this day I'm not sure which designation better describes it. Not only was the building called an apartment house by its tenants, but it was just two blocks from the wide and showy boulevard of tasteful shops and well-appointed buildings called—with a certain glorious civic hyperbole—the Grand Concourse. A kind of Jewish Champs Elysées, the Grand Concourse was the pride and boast of the dentists, furriers, dress manufacturers, and other assorted burghers who dwelled in its lavish apartment houses.

We still formally lived on the wrong side of the official dividing line between the East and West Bronx. That border was Jerome Avenue, along whose entire miles-long extent a branch of the Interborough Rapid Transit, paradoxically known as the elevated subway, or el, blocked out all but the most minimal sunlight even on the brightest days. Still, being so close to the Concourse lessened the distinction considerably. To move to such an area was a statement of optimism, I would realize in later years, that was not only inconsistent with the family's characteristic pessimism but also with its actual financial circumstances. Paid jointly from the insufficient earnings of my father and Tante Aya, the fifty-five-dollar monthly rent was never easily available when the landlord's agent—a perennially sour-faced old maid who was also the sister-in-law of Goldberg, our landlord—came to collect it on the first of each month. Needless to say, Goldberg himself lived on the Grand Concourse and was never seen by any tenant of our building.

In terms of both demographics and geography, our block was informally divided into two almost equal halves, upper and lower. The upper half was Jewish and the lower Gentile. At the southeast corner of 183rd Street and Morris Avenue stood a small, cluttered grocery store run by a Jewish family named Bleifer. But northward from Bleifer's, the lower half of the block was taken up by a row of four one-family brick houses in which *di Irisheh* lived. Ours was, for the most part, an immigrant neighborhood, so "Irish" almost always meant that the parents or at least the grandparents spoke with a heavy brogue. Most of the adults in the families that we called *di Talener,* on the opposite side of the street, had the accents of their Sicilian origins.

Number 2314 lay just north of these houses, at the very center of the block. Adjoining it was a wide dirt lot, on which stood a small wooden building used as a synagogue (or shul), and then an abandoned single-family house. The last structure on the block was a large apartment building on the northeast corner. The abandoned house was destroyed by fire when I was about eight, and the charred remains were left untouched for several years before an apartment building was constructed on the lot it shared with the shul.

All the buildings on the opposite side of the street were apartment houses except for a wooden one-family dwelling near the middle of the block. In the manner of the period, four of the apartment houses were designated not only by street numbers but by proper names as well: They were the Pershing (at 2295), the Funston (2301), and the Dodds (2307), and then, unaccountably, Shari at 2317—three American notables and presumably the daughter of the house's builder. On both sides of the street, the lower half of the block was almost completely Catholic—Irish and Italian—while the upper half was virtually all Jewish. Our building straddled the border. For reasons beyond memory, I played exclusively with "them" until Alfred Salemme and I got into a fistfight with anti-Semitic overtones when I was seven, resulting in a precipitous transfer of my allegiances from the Catholic Rudy's Gang to the predominantly Jewish Popeye's Gang up the block. To us kids, the word *gang* had no dark connotations. It simply meant that a large group of boys played together under the leadership of a particularly gifted athlete. Our leaders were Rudolph Speziale (always called "Rudy Special") and Ronald ("Popeye") Eisenberg.

Morris Avenue in daylight hours was a sea of children of all ages. Shortly after school let out at three o'clock each afternoon, the houses on both sides of the block disgorged dozens of energetic, noisy boys, who quickly joined together in several age-determined groups and started up the round of those games now so well remembered by hundreds of thousands of us who grew up in the boroughs of New York City in the 1930s and 1940s—stickball, punch-ball, johnny-on-the-pony, street hockey on roller skates, baseball against the wall (our version of a sport elsewhere called stoopball), immies (marbles, to the sophisticated), skelly, territory, touch foot-ball, chicken fighting—or just hung around.

Chicken fighting had nothing to do with chickens. It was a challenge of single combat, in which each of the two gladiators would fold both arms across his chest and repeatedly throw him-self forcefully against the front of his opponent while hopping on one leg. The off-balance bumping and banging went on until one of them fell or had to set his raised foot on the pavement in order to stay upright. Sometimes three or more boys took part in the contest, and the winner was the last one of them left hopping.

I missed Rudy's Gang at first, mostly because I had learned so much from the uncensored conversations I heard. Even when not engaged in games, this group of boys always seemed to have tantalizing things to talk about, like the skimpiness of Rosemary O'Sullivan's blue underpants when Frankie Vitagliano caught a glimpse of them as she lost her balance and fell over while playing potsy; or the impressive size of the burgeoning new tits on Jack O'Brien's big sister; or the rumor that Civiletti the shoemaker had been seen in the vestibule of 2295 with his hand up the dress of a giggling Mrs. Cyzmanski, the leggy, bleached-blond wife of our milkman.

Popeye's Gang was more interested in sports, movies, and radio programs than in earthiness. It was with them that I began to engage in endless debates about baseball, although I knew very little about it at first, other than the familiar names of such Yankees as Crossetti, Ruffing, Gomez, Dickey, Rolfe, and the newcomer, DiMaggio. But there would be other ways to continue my education in dirty words and body parts. When I was nine, a super's son, called Fatso, taught me the word *prick* (for months, I thought it was *brick,* to the great amusement of the rest of the guys). He told me what a prick was for—other than pissing through—and at first I had trouble believing it, especially because I had not yet mastered the intricacies of female anatomy, other than to know that girls were prickless. But then I learned *fuck* from another boy, and things made more sense, although it was unimaginable that fucking was actually done by the adults I knew, especially my parents. For about a year, I remained convinced that its purpose was recreational and that only reprehensible teenagers engaged in it. Certainly none of them were Jewish.

It was Fatso who taught me what "scum bags" were used for, those elongated little balloons we would occasionally find in the gutter on summer mornings, through whose astonishingly thin and transparent rubber the compressed foamy fluid of the previous night's fucking could still be seen. He warned me never to touch them, for fear of acquiring the dreadful affliction he ominously called "the clap," or an even worse one, "the syph." Fatso was unable to provide the clinical details of either except to assure me that they involved the prick in some pestilentially destructive way. Of course, in order for me to comprehend what all of this was about, he first had to take me one early evening into the alleyway leading to his parents' flat and there provide me with a detailed description of his version of what actually happened during a fuck, which was much more graphic than the other boy's explanation. His imaginative portrayal of the supposed events all but convinced me that such an awkward coupling could take place only in Fatso's foul and overheated imagination. But I could not entirely dismiss the possibility of its being real, because that might explain some things I had heard Harvey talking about to his friends—not to mention certain peculiar feelings that I was beginning to notice in myself when in the presence of some of the teenage girls on the block. My skepticism ended a year later, when it was reported by a kid whose snoopiness had long since earned him the nickname of "Eyes" that the sixteen-year-old Joe Arizzi was doing It with (or to—I couldn't be sure which) the redheaded, plump-assed Eileen Walsh, whose family of two usually drunk adults and three or four raucous kids lived in the basement flat at 2423.

Our four-room apartment was located on the first floor of 2314, and it was reached by climbing a flight of stairs leading from the street to a locked glass door separating the building's lobby from the outside. A key or buzzer system was required to open the door, but by the time I was ten, I had learned to unlock it with my thumbnail. Once having passed through the door, apartment A, where we lived, was found immediately on the left, at the top of three steps.

The windows of our two bedrooms (Tante Aya and Bubbeh in one, my parents in the other; Harvey and I slept in different places at different times—either in a bedroom or in the living room) fronted on Morris Avenue, though the view from my parents' bedroom was partially blocked by a large fire escape. The windows of the kitchen and living room, on the other hand, faced on the opposite side of the building. They looked out onto the concrete pavement of the back-yard, which was separated by a low stone wall from the adjacent lot, on which stood the synagogue (called "sinigarden" by my father) and the abandoned house. In those first years of living at 2314 Morris Avenue and especially later, when the backyard had been closed in by the construction of the new apartment house, I inadvertently studied sociology and contemporary cultural history just by listening to the conversations and other sounds that wafted unbidden through the open windows of our apartment.

Into that busy little enclosure would come an endless stream of old-clothes peddlers, street singers, itinerant tradesmen of various sorts, and other representatives of that entire spectrum of penny hucksters who made their precarious livings by working the backyards of the Bronx in the decades on either side of World War II. The little courtyard had the acoustic qualities of a vertical sound chute five stories high. On summer days, amplified words flew in and out of open windows as though the speakers intended that their conversation should reach the most remote corner of every neighbor's rooms.

Thanks to a constantly bickering couple on the third floor, I had enlivened my vocabulary with a goodly store of old-world maledictions before my eighth birthday. The acrimonious Weinstein and his acid-tongued missus lived with their retarded adult daughter, Sophie, in a state of perpetual warfare, which made my own family seem like an assemblage of cooing turtledoves. Although they were not particularly innovative in their verbal assaults on one another, their mutuality of eye-bulging animus could be depended upon to provide frequent bursts of the more common Yiddish execrations, in which the dull but nevertheless shrill Sophie was often a participant. Being much taken, even when so young, with forms that I would later learn were called alliteration and parallelism, I was especially fond of *"a brannt dir in di kishkes, a bruch dir in di gedayrim"* ("May there be by you a burning in the intestines, a breaking in the guts"). Though I heard it often, it was not until medical school that I learned that the elder Weinsteins were wishing a case of cholera on each other, a disease well known to the Jews of Eastern Europe. I accumulated a vast store of maledictions like this one, although there are nowadays few opportunities to fling them at deserving recipients who also happen to understand Yiddish.

The sexton of the little shul on the adjoining lot was a short, thin, seemingly perpetually busy man of about my father's age, who scurried endlessly around the wooden building and its surrounding dusty acre during the few hours of the day he was able to spare from whatever was his regular job. I never knew what he did on his nervous errands, but I was sure it must be holy work.

Late one spring Saturday afternoon during my first year in the neighborhood—when I was four—I was playing by myself on the wide expanse of lot just in front of the shul. The bustling little sexton came rushing out in his usual lickety-split way, and then, unaccountably, he stopped still at the top step of the building's porch. He seemed to be looking for someone or something he expected to see in the street. Probably realizing that whatever it was would not be found, he came rushing down the stairs toward me.

"Johnny [the universal name for every *sheygets*, as goyishe boys were called], you vant mek ah penny?"

"Yeh."

"Cahm vid me."

He led me into the shul and picked me up in his arms to reach the light switch.

"Toin on pliz di light."

I did.

"Cahm tamarah in di munnink, Johnny, and I giff you di penny."

Flush with the triumph of my first earned penny, I trundled off at the end of the adventure, eager to tell my parents about the financial bonanza that had befallen me in the very shul where the grown-ups had gone for High Holiday service. Momma looked uneasy as I related my tale of good fortune, probably because she knew what would follow. My father's response was of course predictable. Imagine! A kid from our Orthodox family being used as a Shabbos goy, a Gentile who does Sabbath jobs not permitted to Jews. How could the sexton not know whose son I was? He exploded first at me, then at my mother, and finally rushed off to find the unsuspecting miscreant. He would avenge a personal affront.

Bad enough that the sexton had lifted me up on the Sabbath—

in itself a sin, but one easily rationalized as unavoidable, given the circumstances of his not being able to find his regular Shabbos goy. But of all the kids he might have chosen had he not been in his usual great hurry, he had picked one who was Jewish, and even the child of an observant congregant—an easily enraged one at that, who saw disparagement in every unpleasant encounter. My father's enraged accusation must have spelled out the magnitude of his felony.

The hapless sexton had sinned not only before God but before man as well, and had chosen a son of the wrong man. As ultimately blameless as he was, my pious benefactor must have spent the whole of Saturday night until the dawn in his small wooden shul, reading psalms in the traditional Jewish rite of expiation. As for me, I never did get that penny.

V

An unexpected dividend of my friendships with the boys in Popeye's Gang would occur every Friday afternoon at the beginning of Shabbos, the Sabbath. Whereas extricating myself from the doings of Rudy's Gang had often been difficult at those times, Popeye, Lenny, Herby, and the others understood what had to be done. When the sun began to fade just the least bit, these kids assumed that I would have to quit playing and go home to begin Shabbos, because so many of them did the same. Daddy had a foolproof method of getting me home in a hurry, though he had no idea what he was doing.

Meyer Nudelman believed that certain words were to be heard by the ears of Jews only, for the reason that they would be incomprehensible to anyone else, and mark the speaker as being insufficiently American. Not only that; they would sound too Yiddish. In his calculus of linguistics, therefore, it was necessary to translate such words into a vocabulary that he conceived to be sufficiently sophisticated for general use in the greater society. He never said the word *Passover*, for example, when speaking to non-Jews, so certain was he that it was not in the English lexicon. For reasons known only to himself, he had long ago become convinced that he would sound a bit more polished if he referred to this major Jewish holiday in a way he believed comprehensible to goyim. Accordingly, he called Passover "Easter," pronounced *Isterr.*

Daddy did this kind of thing with several other words, too, among the most worthy of note being *gargle. Gargle* must have sounded to him like a Yiddish word. In Meyer Nudelman's self-invented goyish speech, to gargle was to "swenk di tro." He seemed unable to comprehend that he was defeating his own purpose, because he had, in some linguistically tortured way, ordained that *shvenk,* the Yiddish word for "rinse," was in fact English, and therefore much preferable to the Yiddish-sounding *gargle.* And so, one "swenked" the throat when such things were being discussed with outsiders, and Smitty the mailman or Mr. Conn the super was supposed to know what was meant by that. And amazingly, they did.

In the same way, Meyer would never call me Sheppy or Shepsel within the hearing of any but the family or the wide range of Yiddish speakers whom we knew. When we were together within earshot of the American world, he called me Sherwin, which he, of course, pronounced *Shoifn.* Never mind that I was universally called Shep by friends and neighbors, most of whom had no idea that I might possess some other name. I didn't mind the mangling into Shoifn when we were in a situation where I was likely to be unknown, but I hated the sound of it closer to the streets near home.

Daddy's foolproof way of getting me into the house from a street game was initiated in response to the urgencies of one particular Shabbos. On an early Friday evening in the late spring of my eleventh year, he leaned his body out the window as far as his precarious balance would allow and yelled up the block toward our stickball game. In as loud a voice as possible, he called, "Shoifn! Hey, Shoifn!" Not being particularly gifted at sports, I was, as usual, relegated to the deep outfield, where only a prodigious blast by a prodigious batsman might fly far enough to challenge my limited ball-catching skills. This meant that I was at a distance from my father's resolute vocal cords approximately equal to the yardage between four sewers. But as far as it was, the sound of that "Shoifn" nevertheless carried all the way to my lonely outpost and probably beyond, vibrating the eardrums of everyone in the street and those of the neighbors who were hanging out of their windows at that pleasant time of day. In the Bronx of 1941, that amounted to a considerable number. Mortified by the ludicrous sound of my own name, I abandoned my far-flung position and went dashing toward the source of the paternal bellow. I would have done anything in the world to avoid hearing Daddy let loose another Yiddishoid clarion call to Shabbos assembly. Galloping along at high speed, I nevertheless kept my eye fixed on him, so that I might let out a loud yell if I sensed a repetition about to be brought forth. Just as he opened his mouth to blast out the next volley, he must have caught sight of me coming toward him like a thundering rhinoceros. The outburst was aborted. I was in the house and up the stairs in a flash. From then on, I always stayed within easy sight of the windows of our apartment on late Friday afternoons, watching for the emergence of the familiar head. I never wanted to hear the long-distance shout of "Shoifn!" again.

Although it often took some last-minute scampers, I always made sure to be standing alongside with hands and face washed as Bubbeh lighted the Shabbos candles in the six large and two small brass candlesticks she had brought with her from Novaradugk. Two of them, larger than the rest, had belonged to her grandmother. The eight candlesticks, a heavy brass mortar and pestle, and a copper samovar were the only physical heirlooms of centuries of my family's life in Europe. My father had brought nothing.

When Bubbeh lighted the candles, all of us except Daddy stood alongside her to bid the Sabbath enter our home. It was always a hushed moment, sacred more because it was something we did together every week of our lives than because it was ordained by Jewish law. Though a familiar ritual and therefore comforting in its continuity, Bubbeh's candle lighting seemed new each time and to be somehow distinctively hers—a gift she brought us from *der heym* and from within herself.

The candlesticks were placed on the living-room table, which was set against the wall. Bubbeh would light the candles one after another with a single wooden match, then wave her hands in two separate circles over them, three times, in a kind of wafting motion, as though gathering their sanctity into her palms and sweeping it toward herself. As the final circular movement was completed, she brought her hands to her eyes, and with that gesture, she seemed to draw the sanctity to her. Her face thus covered, Bubbeh said the prayer she had learned as a little girl, thanking God for the *mitzvah,* the obligation, to light candles at such a holy time. She would then remove her hands from before her face, and we would see the tiny brilliance of Shabbos shining there in her eyes.

Shortly after the candles had been lighted, the long table on which they stood would be moved to the center of the room, covered with a freshly laundered and ironed white cloth, and set for dinner. Folding chairs were placed around it, and within an hour or two we would sit down to eat a meal meant to be a ritual celebration of our joy at the arrival of the day of rest. My father sat at the head, with Momma at his right and me at his left. Harvey and Tante Aya sat along either side, and Bubbeh was at the other end of the table. She and Momma would rise from time to time to bring the hot chicken noodle soup or the boiled chicken or the compote or applesauce we had for dessert. We never recited the Kiddush, the blessing over wine that was to have preceded the meal, nor did we read the prayers traditionally said after it. Our Friday-evening piety seemed to have limits when it fell to my father to lead the observance.

Daddy's was a faith of the automatic sort, or perhaps "unthinking" might be a better description of what it really was. If skill at Hebrew prayer means the ability to race mechanically through the liturgy at express-train speed, Daddy was its most accomplished practitioner. But if a sense of wonder, of genuine feeling, were chosen to be the criteria, my father would have come up short. He would have come up short, too, in depth of understanding or even of caring much about his religion's intellectual philosophy or its treasure of symbolism. His approach to Judaism was hardly scholarly, nor was it spiritual.

After our first year in the neighborhood and until my Bar Mitzvah—when our allegiance was transferred to the grander Concourse Center of Israel—Daddy would attend services on the High Holidays and only occasionally on a Shabbos morning (with me reluctantly in tow) in a run-down storefront shul about two blocks away. It was located on Walton Avenue, just around the corner from the bustling food market where Momma bought her Shabbos chicken every Friday morning. Later in the day, the bird would be boiled in water with three cents' worth of greens to make chicken soup. When eaten that evening, it was as flat and spiritless as those formalized prayers that rat-tat-tatted from Daddy's lips.

I would later realize that my father's old-world Hebrew education had been skimpy and concentrated only on the ability to fulfill the requirements of rote ritual. To him, meaning was of far less importance than correct performance and kosher food. Looking back on it, I find myself doubting that he really thought much about belief. In fact, he rarely went to the synagogue except on the High Holidays, when the stakes were high. He prayed without questioning, because that is what Jews do; he prayed without questioning, because to do otherwise was to risk the wrath of a God who takes vengeance if a single Hebrew sentence goes unsaid or a word is misspoken in the service; and he prayed without questioning, because his father—the father he had left behind in the shtetl so many years earlier—had demanded it of him on countless Shabbos mornings in a small Novoselitz synagogue.

The reverberations of my father's particular form of unquestioning religiosity are with me still. At the best of times, they have been the stuff of nostalgia; at the worst of times, they have been demons besetting my mind. At a particular moment on every Rosh Hashanah and Yom Kippur morning, I still call my children's attention to the dread-inspiring prayer that is about to be recited on that solemn day of divine judgment and atonement for sin. I do it as a kind of memorial to my father, because he would invariably poke me in the side at that dramatic point in the service, to be sure that I was aware of its towering significance in the life of every Jew. Though I have come to think of the prayer, called Untaneh Tokef, as a kind of metaphor for morality, it was not always so. In my blackest days of depression, the imagery and connotations of its three vivid paragraphs were the stuff of some of my most consuming obsessions. Some brooding part of my consciousness believed in their literal meaning:

> We will observe the mighty holiness of this day, for it is one of awe and anxiety. Thereon is Thy dominion exalted. On this day we conceive Thee established on Thy throne of mercy, sitting thereon in truth. We behold Thee, as Judge and Witness, recording our secret thoughts and acts and setting the seal thereon. Thou recordest everything; yea, Thou rememberest the things forgotten. Thou unfoldest the records, and the deeds therein inscribed tell their own story, for lo, the seal of every man's hand is set thereto.
>
> The great Shofar is sounded, and a still small voice is heard. The angels in heaven are alarmed and are seized with fear and trembling, as they proclaim "Behold the Day of Judgment!" The hosts of heaven are to be arraigned in judgment, for in Thine eyes even they are not free from guilt. All who enter the world dost Thou cause to pass before Thee, one by one, as a flock of sheep. As a shepherd musters his sheep and causes them to pass beneath his staff, so dost Thou pass and record, count and visit,

every living soul, appointing the measure of every creature's life and decreeing its destiny.

> *On Rosh Hashanah it is written*
> *and on Yom Kippur it is sealed:*

> *How many shall leave this world and how many shall be born into it: who shall live and who shall die; who shall live out the limit of his days and who shall not; who shall perish by fire and who by water; who by sword and who by beast; who by hunger and who by thirst; who by earthquake and who by plague; who by strangling and who by stoning; who shall rest and who shall wander; who shall be at peace and who shall be tormented; who shall be poor and who shall be rich; who shall be humbled and who shall be exalted.*

> *But penitence, prayer and good deeds can avert the severity of the decree.*

When I am nowadays most adamant in my rejection of the notion of supernatural forces—of the existence of God, in fact—it is because I have never completely lost a lingering fear of the seductive power of theology like that expressed in the Untaneh Tokef. It has been for me like the song of the Lorelei, trying to lure me back to the destructive reefs of obsessional thinking, guilt, and depression. This is the heritage I have carried, the legacy of the formalized religion of my father, and no doubt also of the superstition of my Bubbeh.

But there is another side to it. Formalized religion, formalized prayer, formalized observance—they are all part of the heritage of my family, and I cherish the sustenance they give me. More than cherish—I *need* it. As agnostic as my philosophy is, the synagogue has been a place of refuge and a home for me, and the congregation a family. With my wife and my children, I go there more than occasionally, a skeptic faithful to his memories.

Bubbeh's Jewishness, unlike Daddy's, was of a deeply spiritual sort, though she had no formal schooling. Hers was a homogeneous blending of religion, old-world superstition, and folklore, and its elements were inseparable. Her relationship to God was so personal that she often addressed Him in the diminutive, as did other shtetl women of her generation. He was Gotenyu, "my adored Goddy," as though she were speaking directly to one of her beloved grandchildren, but one with all the direction of the universe contained in His powerful goodness. She believed with an intensity that guided her life and enabled her to endure in the face of tragedy after tragedy. My father, on the other hand, believed because he was a Jew, and Jews are expected to believe, at least on Rosh Hashanah and Yom Kippur, when fate and destiny are determined. For this reason, he rattled out the prayer without thought—unless it was of the magnitude of Untaneh Tokef—and admonished his sons to do the same, lest some awfulness befall them.

On Friday evenings, what should have been a weekly meal of celebration was instead a strained hour in one another's company. My father rarely interrupted his loud, openmouthed chewing to say more than a brief sentence, almost always directed at Momma, almost always in the form of an order, and almost always for more food or a refilling of his water glass. Anything else he said was almost always an admonition to Harvey or me about some transgression in the way we were eating. Bubbeh and Tante Aya hardly spoke, either to each other or to the rest of us.

In fact, my father never actually asked for more water. His way was to slide his empty glass toward my place, which I was to interpret as a signal to take it to the kitchen for refilling. When I reached my teens, I would torment him by ignoring its presence in front of me, as though to transmit the message that I deserved the

courtesy of being asked to get more water. These little perform-
ances would on each occasion become a minor battle of wills, always
ending when Daddy abruptly raised the tumbler a few inches and
then slammed it down on the tabletop with a loud bang. I would
unfailingly give in at that point.

In all of this, the Friday-evening meal was no different from the
suppers we ate on any day of the week, except that the others were
served in the kitchen.

But on Friday evenings, the atmosphere lightened as soon as
the Shabbos meal was over. The table was cleared and put back in
its place against the far wall, the dishes and pots were washed in
the sink and dried with a cloth towel, and my father sat down to
read the *Daily Forward*. By 8:00 p.m., people would begin to arrive,
and the talking started up.

Long before I had learned to read, my stories from the world
came to me through the lips of the many relatives and *landsleit*
who gathered in our small apartment on Friday evenings, an hour
or so after the Shabbos meal, to pay a kind of matriarchal court to
Bubbeh. No one called in advance, and no one owned a car. They
would arrive by trolley, by bus, and by subway, and some would
walk miles to be there. Even at the age of three or four, I would sit
on the floor near Bubbeh as their multiple conversations whirled
around my head—talk of the old country, of people, of events, of
misfortunes, and of happiness. Though none of my father's family
was ever there, he was always part of it, in spite of speaking not a
word to Bubbeh or Tante Aya. They were in the same room, but he
acted oblivious to their existence, and they, in turn, ignored his
presence even as he conversed with their visitors. It was Bubbeh's
world for those hours, and Daddy never intruded his needs into
it. He seemed to be enjoying himself, and not feeling at all like an
outsider.

But at most other times, things were different. No matter the
constancy of the contempt to which he was subjected by Bubbeh

and Tante Aya, the ever-present threat of Daddy's volcanic temper assured him a certain suzerainty over the atmosphere of our home. Each of us was afraid of him, and each of us coped with it in a different way. Momma seemed reconciled to the difficulty of preventing his rages, but she had long ago learned to avoid certain sensitive topics. We two boys accommodated by treading softly around him, never certain when he might take offense at a remark meant only to be jocular. We had no way of knowing when some perfectly innocuous comment might prove to hold within it a meaning or even a tone in which he could identify an unintended diminishment of his authority. His sensitivity to the older women's attitude toward him only reinforced his determination to maintain dominion over all of us, as though to suppress any hint that he was not the controlling influence over our lives.

Daddy's brooding hegemony was lessened for a while when Tante Beattie died, sometime after my ninth birthday. She was thirty-eight years old, and the fourth of Bubbeh's children to lose her life in the golden land of America. None of the others had reached their late twenties. Beattie left her eleven-year-old daughter, Arline—or Elke Dveyreh, as the adults called her—to be raised by her mother and sisters. Her fatal illness was Bright's disease, at the time a not uncommon process of progressive destruction of the kidneys. It usually was precipitated by an undiagnosed and unremembered streptococcal sore throat, going on to cause renal poisoning and gradual failure. Its relentless advance toward an inevitable death took place over the course of years or even decades. No one knew when Beattie's illness had begun.

In the days after Beattie's funeral, Uncle Manny, her husband, became distraught beyond even the sorrow of his wife's early death, and some of it was my fault. Arline had been taken out of the funeral chapel just before the announcement was made that the mourners might file past the open coffin for a final good-bye before the lid was sealed. When on the morning after burial Arline asked me what had been going on during the brief interval while she was outside in the hallway, I foolishly told her—without stopping to consider how she might react to knowing. As might have been predicted by anyone but me, she became hysterical with the grief of being the one person deprived of seeing her mother's face for one last time. Hot tears pouring down her cheeks, she ran screaming into the arms of her father, who had been sitting on a low stool in the living room, trying to distract himself from his own anguish and everyone else's by riffling through the pages of the *Daily News*. He became enraged at what Arline told him I had said, and instead of trying to comfort her, he arose from his seat, his fury compounded by what must have been the frustration of having lost control over the circumstances in which his own daughter was living. "THIS IS A CRAZY HOUSE!" he roared, flinging the tabloid to the floor and thumping heavily out of the living room and into the kitchen. He slammed the framed-glass door of the room behind him, and the air seemed to tremble in the wake of his anger and my sudden mortifying realization of how stupid I had been—and my fear of retribution.

Worse than Manny's words was their obvious meaning. "Crazy" referred not to that moment or those events, but to everything about us, and each person mourning in that room must have known it exactly as I knew it. In those few words, he denounced us as people who behaved like no one else, who did everything wrong, who had no connection to the ways in which real human beings lived their lives, who were different from all other families. It was a global condemnation of everything we were, coming from the only member of our extended family whom we thought of as worldly. I had known it before, but I knew it now in a new form, from the lips of a man who understood these things. Manny had long cultivated an air of righteous and knowing authority among us, and to be excoriated by him was to be judged by one elevated, who saw us as we were, as we would be seen through the eyes of any sensible person out there in that world understood by none of us.

That moment is only one of my memories of the days after Beattie died. Though I had heard many times of the deaths of my grandfather, Aunt Annie, and my two uncles soon after their arrival on the shores of the Promised Land—and of Maishele's death, too—hers was the first I had experienced. Beattie's shiva, the seven days of mourning prescribed by Jewish law, pervaded apartment A with a gloom so heavy and palpable, it was as though we were submerged within a sombrous gray cloud of stifling miasma. Except for my father, who was not a blood relative, the grown-ups sat on low stools or orange crates obtained for the purpose from Harry Rivkin's Fruit and Vegetable Market on 183rd Street. They walked about the apartment in stocking feet or flat slippers, symbolically denying themselves the comforts of ordinary living. Mirrors were enshrouded in large bedsheets to prevent the vanity of seeing a reflected face. Uncle Manny did not shave. Beyond the most rudimentary ablutions, no one bathed. Beattie's shiva was sackcloth and ashes; it was the sound of muffled sobs, echoing down through the generations of our family.

But even all of this could not account for the full extent of Uncle Manny's reaction to his wife's death. I tried to liken it to the grief of Bubbeh, Momma, and Tante Aya, but I could not. He seemed to alternate between moroseness and anger. There was something about the way he looked and the way he sounded that placed him at a remoteness from the rest of us, of a sort quite different from the distance at which my father was removed.

Uncle Manny's body was of a type that tailors of that time called "portly." As with many bulky men, a solidly protruding belly and thick, wide shoulders made him appear larger and more physically imposing than his modest height—which was the same as my father's—would have justified. He combed his thinning brown hair very carefully across his broad, sparsely covered pate, leaving a wide bald spot far back. This, along with the rectangular frameless glasses he wore, his thick, dark mustache, and an ever-present cigar, gave him somewhat an air of urbanity, which he cultivated in our presence, as though in a constant state of informing us—hopeless shtetl Jews that we were—of his lofty eminence in our midst. As if my father's situation were not precarious enough, Daddy suffered even more by the unspoken comparison to the worldly-wise and Viennese-born Emanuel Ritter, with his knowing air of superior wisdom. In the presence of that august personage, everyone was somewhat diminished, Daddy by much more than the rest of us. He had to defer to him, and hold his unrestrained moods in check when Manny was in the house. During the following two years, Manny's presence there was far more than any of us would have liked.

Merely to speak unaccented English and no Yiddish would have been credentials enough to substantiate his elevated status. But Uncle Manny was possessed of the pinnacle of bona fides: He worked in an office—not in a sweatshop or its equivalent, where so many of the Jews we knew did work, but in an actual office. I would learn in later years that his job was not much higher than a secretary's, but by then it did not matter, because I had long since discovered that his loftiness was without substance.

My father and Manny had virtually nothing in common. They were odd bedfellows, thrown together only because they had married sisters. I never saw them alone together but once. It was during Tante Beattie's shiva.

All three of us were taking a head-clearing walk a few blocks up Morris Avenue, probably trying to escape the oppressive mood of the long days of mourning. It was two days after Manny's outburst. I was walking several paces in front of the two men, straining to eavesdrop on their conversation, while at the same time staying as far from them as I could. I heard enough to know that they were exchanging confidences, an unprecedented thing in my experience of them, especially in light of Uncle Manny's clear majesty over my father and his generally condescending approach to him. I was catching only bits of sentences, when all at once Manny's voice rose in indignation, and he growled something loudly enough for it to reach my ears in its entirety: "You'd think they'd tell you their daughter was sick before they let you marry her!" Daddy mumbled something in reply, which I took to be an assent, making me assume that Manny was referring to Momma. But as I caught bits of subsequent sentences, I realized that he was talking about himself and Tante Beattie. Astoundingly, he was saying that he would not have married her had he known of the Bright's disease.

Until that moment, it had never entered my head that the married people in my family had not been joined together because fate predestined it and they desired such permanence. Although I had seen plenty of movies, movies had nothing to do with the lives of people like Nudelmans and Lutskys. I had heard of divorce, and I even knew that men and women *choose* to marry, but these things seemed not to apply to the lives of the people from whom I sprang. Such considerations were for others, those who lived out there in the American world and could be seen in movies. They, the vast majority, had nothing to teach us, because we were too immersed in our immigrant Jewishness to learn from them. We were creatures of a different sort. Our lot was to be trapped in our everyday lives, to inhabit always a world of unhappiness and be swept up in the ominous tides of those misfortunes that would surely come tomorrow. The elders among us stayed together, it seemed, because that was the nature of their lives. Bubbeh and Tante Aya manifestly had only disdain for my father, and he, in turn, despised them, and yet I never heard a word, an intimation, that the three of them might not remain in the same household. I was never threatened by that possibility. Disagreement and sometimes bitterness were the coin of ordinary conversation between my parents, but the two of them remained solidly linked, as though an inseparable bond of perpetual low-level tension was necessary—was an ingredient of the glue that held them together, or an expression of a uniquely Jewish kind of love. Or at least I saw it that way.

At the age of nine, I assumed that all Jewish husbands spoke to their wives in the brusque way Daddy often spoke to Momma; I assumed that all Jewish wives put up with grumbling and chronic anger about petty things, as Momma did. This was the unchanging nature of their lives. I had almost never seen tenderness pass between them, and yet I did not doubt the permanence of their commitment to each other.

Even Bubbeh and Tante Aya seemed to have some unknowable festering grudge that poisoned the air between them, and only Momma could mediate it. And yet, they never separated.

The reason I had thought that Uncle Manny was referring to my mother when he complained about his ignorance of Beattie's condition was because of an enigmatic illness, whose symptoms Momma had already been exhibiting for several years at the time of her sister's death. I had only a muddled idea of what it might be. I knew merely that I had heard it called "woman's sickness" by Daddy in hushed conversation one evening with his friend Dudie Polishook. Dudie was my father's fellow lodge member in a Jewish fraternal organization, Novoselitzer Progressive Branch 498 of the Workmen's Circle, and a man admired for his sober judgment and ability to keep confidences. He had nodded knowingly on being given the information and silently taken a few puffs on his ever-present pipe, staring at the floor all the while in deep concentration. Because he had a reflective demeanor, thick steel gray hair that he combed straight back from his forehead, bushy brows, and a preternaturally deep, slow voice, I was certain that his unspoken concurrence meant that my father must know what he was talking about. This was an unusual thing for me, to acknowledge that Daddy's interpretation of events was based on any real understanding or knowledge. Had Dudie's response not added weight to my father's explanation of Momma's mysterious problem, I would have given it no credence, which was my usual way of dealing with Meyer Nudelman's opinions about matters that required worldly information and wisdom.

"Woman's sickness" meant that Momma had something wrong in a "down below" place, whose exact nature was obscure. The secret of that place's precise location and its function were beyond my understanding, but not beyond their ability to make me apprehensive. The unknowable female place between the legs was somehow dirty and surely played a part in the foul doings that Fatso had surreptitiously told me about in that alleyway introduction to reproductive physiology.

From time to time, I saw thick gauze pads in the bathroom just before they were thrown out. They would be drenched in drying reddish brown fluid, which seemed a repulsive form of diseased blood. Long before I heard my father's comment to Dudie, I had asked my P.S. 33 friend Jerry Kass if he knew the possible source of such apparently discharged stuff, and he had told me that his tall, ginger-haired mother experienced the same thing for a few days each month and he believed that all other women did, too. But the origins of Jerry's movie-star beautiful mom were Scandinavian, and the Kasses owned a car, lived in a modern apartment house with an elevator, and went on picnics, at which they cooked hamburgers on outdoor grills in the parks of Westchester County, so Momma could not possibly have the same thing happening to her. And also, there was the additional fact that Momma's pads would appear at any time and far more frequently than a few days a month. More often than not, they smelled bad. I was sure she had something nasty going on in that "down below" place and that it was unique to her.

Periodically, perhaps once or twice a year, the inscrutable illness became severe enough that Momma had to go into the hospital for a week or more. About ten years earlier, my father's cousin Willie Nudelman—the son of the uncle with whom Daddy had lived on first arriving in America—had renamed himself Nuland and gone off to Switzerland to become a doctor. In those days of Jewish quotas in university admissions, this was not an uncommon thing to do. Internships being hard to come by for a student with a foreign degree, Willie had, after much searching, found one at the 160-bed Beth David Hospital, located on East Ninetieth Street in Manhattan. When Momma needed hospitalization, she would be admitted to Beth David, and Willie would arrange for her to be seen on the regular rounds of medical school–affiliated specialists who were consultants there. "Willie the doctor," as my father admiringly called him, was a man we were all very proud of, including Bubbeh and Tante Aya. Although Daddy and Willie were first cousins, Willie, for official purposes, would tell people that my father was his uncle and that he was mine. That small subterfuge made things easier when we needed help with one or another medical problem, which was more often than any of us would have liked.

Willie put himself through college by playing the saxophone in dance bands, but he had the bad timing to graduate in the 1930s, when the sons of Eastern European Jews were having particularly great difficulties in being admitted to medical school. His father barely made a living, and that compounded the problem. But just at this point, Willie met the vivacious red-haired daughter of a housepainter, fell in love, and married, which immediately improved his fortunes. To families as poor as his, a housepainter was considered a well-off man, and this one was openhanded. But an artisan's means during the Depression were not large; there were limits to how much he could help the young couple. So, with saxophone and bride, Willie took himself to Lausanne to study medicine, supplementing his father-in-law's periodic checks with as many gigs as he could get. After graduation and internship, he settled in the Bronx to practice; except for his war years in the South Pacific, he was our doctor. He charged us what we could afford to pay, which was nothing.

Willie was the youngest of the four children of my great-uncle, and Daddy had doted on him since he was a small boy. He grew up to be as generous and loyal as he was brash and outspoken, and he never forgot the kindness of his much older greenhorn cousin, Meyer. This kindness was a side of Daddy that his own family saw only in brief moments, but to Willie, who had known him during his vibrant and optimistic youth, this was the Meyer Nudelman he remembered and understood. He considered it his obligation to watch over all of us.

A desolation overtook Daddy each time Momma had to go into the hospital. He would become subdued, and the threat of his possible displeasure would ebb with his waning spirits. He became more solicitous of Harvey and me. When I took my weekly bath, he would come in like Momma did and try to help me wash. But he never knew how to do it and his efforts were clumsy. I knew that he wanted very much to do what he could for me, and I also knew that I had to let him try. Even his cabinet-slamming and foot-stomping ceased, and the kitchen encounters with Bubbeh became suddenly uneventful. A part of him seemed to be missing. He walked around as though bewildered sometimes, and could not understand what was happening.

Beth David did not allow children under the age of twelve to visit. Daddy would take Harvey and me to the hospital by subway, and the two of them would then go upstairs, leaving me outside by myself. One of those images that have remained with me through these many years is of a boy of eight and then nine and then ten standing alone on the sidewalk across the street from the six-story hospital and looking up at his mother's window on the third floor.

I would wave to her again and again, and she would wave back. I cannot now remember how many visits or how many hospitalizations occasioned this scene, but for at least a week or two each year, it would be my only contact with Momma. I never cried.

Until an appendectomy just before my tenth birthday, I had no idea what went on in a hospital, other than my confused memories of my stay in Willard Parker. But I did understand that Momma was always tired and sick when she entered, then always seemed much better when she returned home. And each time, she would become my mommy again—kind and patient and wise, as though we had never been apart and she had never been sick. And even when she got tired again, she was never too tired for me.

A few months after my tenth birthday, in December of 1940, Momma's sickness worsened. She became easily exhausted, and her features were by then noticeably puffy. There were more pads and more mess—and more smell, too. There were several more hospitalizations, but now Momma did not return to her old self when they were over. When she came home after the last one, in the fall of 1941, her skull was distorted by an asymmetrical swelling, and her face was bloated. Outpatient X-ray treatments to her head were begun, but they succeeded only in causing large swatches of hair to fall out. Her skull became more misshapen than ever. Even in the house, she took to wearing a scarf wound like a turban around her head, to hide the bare and thinned places on her scalp. Her voice was weak and high-pitched. It had lost the melodious and nurturing mother-sound that until those days had accompanied my life.

And then one day, Momma looked up from the bed she had shared with Daddy since their marriage, and something wondrous passed between them. It was the most natural moment, the only truly lovely one, I had ever witnessed in all the years of living so close to them and observing their contentious behavior. I was standing in the doorway to the bedroom, where Momma now spent almost all of every day, but they seemed not to be aware of my presence. "How can you still care for me," she asked of him in Yiddish, "when I look like this?" Daddy never took his eyes from hers, and he answered with the words that even at ten I knew she needed to hear: "It was not for your hair that I fell in love with you," he said in the gentlest of voices. Had I not been witness to the many moments of bitterness in all those years of being so close to my mother and father, I might have thought as I stood there a few feet from them that theirs was a great and eternal love and that this was one of its truest moments. Perhaps it was, and perhaps it was.

VI

Toward the end, there was a nurse. I had no idea where she came from, nor could I guess the origin of the money that paid her salary.

Esther was in her late twenties. It may have been her quiet cheerfulness, or the way she handled every small crisis with sweet-tempered imperturbability, but whatever the reason, she brought a new atmosphere into apartment A. Even in the midst of Momma's rapidly increasing frailty and the clinical accompaniments of her illness—soiled dressings and bedsheets, unpleasant odors, and the all-too-obvious suffering—Esther's efficient calm and self-assurance generated an unaccustomed air of order and control, which subtly transformed the mood of every one of us, even in the face of the unfolding events. Though I never thought about it at the time, she must have been a balm to my mother's state of mind. In the presence of such a level-headed woman, any rancor expressed by Bubbeh, Tante Aya, and my father would have been ingratitude— an offense against her kind serenity.

It was not as though the suspension of the usual simmering bitterness was deliberate. It came about without forethought; it simply arrived with Esther and stayed, not only during the ten hours of her regular daily shift but all the rest of the time, too. Her effect was felt even when she was not physically among us.

With Esther there, the everyday events surrounding Momma's illness seemed somehow unthreatening and manageable. The penumbra of her comforting influence sheltered me from turmoil and maintained the regularity of my life. She probably did the same for Harvey at fourteen and Arline at twelve, but as she watched over me, I could think of her only as mine. No doubt she watched over Bubbeh and Tante Aya, too—and perhaps especially over Daddy, the one of us who appeared to be the most bewildered and unable to cope as Momma's symptoms worsened. He seemed not to know how to help, either himself or anyone else. He sat, and he stood, and he wandered aimlessly about the apartment, as though seeking some tranquil place where he might lose awareness of everything going on around him. I wonder now whether he had, any more than I, a real comprehension of the finality that all of us were unwilling to face.

Esther's equanimity tranquilized my perception of everything I saw during those weeks. Momma was sicker than she had ever been, and physically altered in a way that was grotesquely unlike her. And yet, I never thought in terms of losing her. It could not enter my mind that she was near death. I would go in and out of her room and talk to her as I always had, about ordinary things, like my schoolwork or a radio program I had heard. After the December 7 attack on Pearl Harbor, I avoided any mention of the war, because I had been told it would upset her. Though she looked vastly changed and sounded vastly changed, she was my mommy, and in this there could be no change. Even the visible evidence was not enough to make me think that my mother was dying. And, of course, the grown-ups did not speak of it.

In spite of all the deaths in our family, I never considered that such a thing might soon happen to Momma. Nothing would prepare me for its possibility; the calculus of my understanding had no formula for it. Momma was an eternal presence in my life, and such certainties do not cast themselves to the winds, even in the face of dreadful illness and unremitting testimonies to the inevitable. In spite of everything I saw him doing and not doing as he went about the apartment perennially lost, I never realized that my father was as unprepared as I.

I returned from school on an overcast afternoon a week after my eleventh birthday—the date was Tuesday, December 16, 1941—to find that my father and Tante Aya were at home. For the first time in my recollection, neither of them had gone to work that morning, but I had not allowed myself to guess why. I had not seen Momma before going off to P.S. 33, but it was hardly the first time that such a thing had happened. But circumstances were clearly different on that leaden-gray late fall afternoon. Still, it was only when Daddy told me that I was not to go to Hebrew School that the sudden realization struck home, after all the avoidance of the weeks leading up to it: This was the day that my mother would die.

All of us were gathered together in the living room, several short steps from the closed door beyond which Esther sat with my mother. Willie arrived about an hour after we three kids had come home from school, and went directly into the bedroom. He stayed a short time, coming out ten minutes later and then leaving after the exchange of a few hushed sentences with my father and then Tante Aya and Bubbeh. But not a word was spoken to Harvey, to Arline, or to me. We dared not ask what was happening. From time to time, one or another of the adults went into the bedroom and remained there awhile, but we kids were told nothing. No conversation included us or passed between us. We were left to our own fears.

Shortly after five o'clock, Esther came out and closed the bedroom door softly behind her. Everyone stood up expectantly, waiting for her to speak. She did not have to say a word—the message was in her face. There was an instant of seemingly shocked disbelief, and then all at once Bubbeh and Tante Aya were shrieking, shouting, crying out the immensity of their grief beyond bearing. My father collapsed into a chair, shoulders heaving uncontrollably with the force of his helpless sobbing. I never looked at Harvey or Arline, but I could hear them softly crying. I must have been the last to react, and it came slowly. No one had explained anything to me or told me—and now Momma was gone from my life. The truth flowed toward me and over me, until I was finally submerged in it.

I never moved from the spot where I had been when Esther entered the room. A huge globular, expanding thing began to fill my chest and throat, pushing itself in all directions, until it stuffed everything out of its way and choked off the air I was trying to breathe—growing more uncontrollably larger and finally overflowing upward into my head and then out through my eyes in great, slow, soundless tears. The tears were followed in a moment by an overwhelming wave of nausea, and then another and another. I rushed into the bathroom, with the worried Esther right behind me, and crouched on my knees over the bowl as my entire insides loudly heaved themselves out and downward toward its depths. The refusal to believe, the despair, the horror, the aloneness— everything I had been holding unacknowledged within me for months—was disgorged violently into the water. Retching and retching in paroxysmal whoops of guttural barking that threw themselves up from an incomprehensible depth, I felt after awhile like even the emptiness was trying to force its way out. I was being scraped raw and turned inside out by the urgency of each spasm, and I could do nothing about it until the series of convulsive outbursts had run the course of their savagery.

Through it all, Esther held my head tightly, her right hand gripping my forehead and her left clasped against the back of my skull. It seemed as if she were trying to keep everything together;

trying to prevent the intensity of the vomiting from shattering my head from within and propelling its fragments of bone, brain, and soul outward in all directions. I was used to the gentle way that my mommy had always held one hand against my forehead when I threw up, but Esther's firm, encircling grip was a new thing, and it felt at once like an unnecessarily constraining vise on my emotions and a needed reassurance.

Finally, the spasms ended and the reality of death and emptiness was the only thing left behind. My mother's advancing sickness had for years been a fact of my life, but her death was something different—a thing hardly contemplated and yet now also a fact. She had been taken away from me, and I was desperate to have her back again. I yearned for today to be yesterday; if I could just return to yesterday, she would still be alive. I could not let my mommy leave me; I would find ways to bring her back.

I remember nothing about the rest of the evening, or that long night.

The funeral the next day was a portrait of anguish. Bubbeh would not be consoled; she was unwilling to listen to words of comfort. She seemed a tiny figure, swollen by her weeping into a presence so formidable that it crowded out the grief of others and made it seem of less consequence than hers. The short funeral service was drenched in her tears. The arms of two *landsleit* were required to hold her up as we left the chapel, and she cried out to the mourners crowded around her on the sidewalk alongside the large black hearse in which Momma's body lay: *"Di oreme yeseymim! Di oreme yeseymim!"* ("The poor orphans! The poor orphans!")

That phrase was the one thing I ever heard Bubbeh say that I resented. And I resented, too, that she seemed able to think only of her own loss and her own way of seeing our family. I was not, after all, an orphan—and I wanted no pity. To Bubbeh, our not having Momma meant our not having parents, as though my father did not exist. But I saw it differently. My life had lost the most important person it would ever know, but this family—as chaotic, unworldly, tragedy-struck, and pessimistic as it might be—was mine, and Momma was still part of it. Her physical presence was no longer with us, but I would not let her leave me. I would see to it that she accompanied me all the days of my life. No, Bubbeh, I thought, I am not an orphan. Whatever my father may be, he is nevertheless my father.

All through the funeral, I felt strangely distanced from everything going on around me. Having sat isolated and silent in the car that took us on the long, slow ride through the now-developing area where I had spent the first three years of my life, then across the Whitestone Bridge, and finally to the Mt. Hebron Cemetery in Queens, I watched almost emotionless as Momma's coffin was lowered into the grave. Daddy stood between Harvey and me, holding each of us to him in a grip so awkwardly tight that I could barely maintain my balance. We let him do what he had to. We knew that he was trying to give us strength.

Before the first shovelful of earth thudded onto the coffin's bare surface, Rose all at once threw herself forward toward the gaping hole in the December-hardened ground, and she would have plunged into it but for the quick response of a tall Nudelman cousin standing near her. He threw his arms over her shoulders from behind, holding on tightly, though she loudly denied what had been her obvious intent. "What do you think I'm going to do," she protested in shouted Yiddish, "throw myself into my sister's grave?" He kept holding her until she stopped straining against his grip and then finally became quiet.

The rabbi took a small knife out of his pocket and cut a slit into the strip of black fabric that a funeral director's assistant had pinned to the clothes of each member of the family except me, because I was not yet old enough to be a part of the formalities of mourning. By Jewish law as by all else, I was set apart from the rest. He then led Harvey and me with difficulty through the words of the Kaddish, the ancient mourner's prayer. Because my father had already told us what obligations lay ahead—and the enormous consequences of not keeping them—the rabbi did not have to admonish us to go to the synagogue to pray at each of the several services conducted every day of the week. We already understood: We were to recite the Kaddish for eleven months as a tribute to Momma, and to ensure her admission into the presence of God. Much depended on the fulfillment of our solemn responsibility.

When all was done, we returned to the funeral director's cars and were taken home to 2314 Morris Avenue, apartment A, to begin the seven-day period known as sitting shiva.

Each of us mourned alone. Bubbeh, Tante Aya, my father, Harvey—all of those who were adults by Jewish law—sat on the sadly familiar orange crates or low stools, getting up only to shuffle in stocking feet or slippers from one room to another, wearing the same clothes day after day and passing the draped mirrors without caring what their reflections might have looked like. Beginning at about noon, visitors were constantly coming and going. Every evening, the house was filled as though for one of Bubbeh's Friday audiences. The conversations were subdued, the mood was desolate, and there was no rousing the three grown-ups from the hopelessness evident in every action they took. In the early part of the day, before company had yet arrived, Daddy had no one to speak to except one or another of us kids. He seemed completely isolated and lost, even more than he had been before Momma's death. He once or twice tried to comfort Harvey and me, but he could not find the right way to do it, any more than he had at the cemetery.

Each of us mourned alone. Everyone in that apartment was steeped in a personal grief that did not admit the others. During the week of shiva, I never heard a word of consolation or support spoken by a single one of the adults to another. Each person was distanced from anything outside of her- or himself. They sat shiva in the grip of private thoughts and private sorrow.

Each of us mourned alone. Except for Daddy's few inept attempts, no one tried to help me through the loss of my momma. I was left to find my own way, and it was to my momma that I turned to seek it. I would do it by insulating myself from everything around me, in order to find her presence to be surrounded with; I would do it by turning inward, where she somehow lived inside me, even as she had all of my life. As desolate and alone as I was, the loneliness of shiva was somehow comforting, because it excluded the world and prevented anything or anyone from intruding on the small universe that came into being when we were together in my thoughts.

It never crossed my mind to think about Daddy's sorrow. He was, after all, a grown man. And I thought grown men could bear everything. That his isolation had become magnified even beyond its usual immensity; that he would now face the rest of his years alone; that he had lost the only person in the world to whom he was able to speak freely, the only person in the world who could mollify his moods or assuage his disappointments and his anger, the only person in the world with whom he had ever been able to share his life—I had no idea of these things, and they would have been meaningless had someone told me about them. I was a boy of eleven and my mother had just died; like everyone else, I could think only of myself.

The seven days of shiva ended on December 22, a Monday. Harvey, Arline, and I stayed out of school for the remaining short period before the start of the Christmas holidays. The prescribed observance was done, the visitors and orange crates disappeared, and the mirrors once again looked out on the rooms of our little apartment, now reflecting a new emptiness. The shining glass revealed the images of three shattered adults and two boys so shaken by their loss that they could not speak about it, even when they were together. Each of them was an island entire of itself—deserted, remote from everything, and without a map or a guide to make sense of the uncertain terrain.

As for Arline, she wandered through her changed life as though on unsteady legs, her stability unsure, her equilibrium barely sustained. She seemed much of the time like a staggering prizefighter, head barely cleared from one blow, only to be hit again by the next. And for her, there would be even more to endure—she was to be taken from us.

Momma's death had provided Uncle Manny with just the pretext he needed, enabling him to carry out a plan he had more than once hinted at during the two years since Arline's arrival at our house. He would move to Brooklyn—on the other side of the city and so far away from us—to be near his own family. Arline was to be brought up in his sister's household. And so, yet another cruelty was inflicted on Bubbeh, barely softened by Manny's promise that her only granddaughter would be allowed—allowed, no less—to visit us every weekend.

I cannot imagine that Daddy was sorry to see his brother-in-law fade from our daily lives. Manny's stature in the household was a constant reproach to him, a continual admonition that he had failed to find his way in America, and that he never would. Having lost so much, Daddy would at least be free of this goading reminder of his inadequacies. But these, too, were things I never thought about. I only now understand them.

I look back on those days as a time of being enwrapped in some kind of invisible insulation. Momma was gone, and yet she was not gone. Everything in the apartment was redolent of her—she was not a memory, but a presence. Every object and every way of doing things was hers, and she was in all of it and in me, as well. I focused inward to keep her with me, as if she would disperse into the surrounding air if I did otherwise. In the warmth and protection of the isolation we shared, Momma and I dwelled within each other, and no other person or thing was permitted to enter, lest something of her be lost. The danger was that the closeness of her presence would come undone and she would be gone from me forever.

I was obsessive in these ruminations. The adults around me must have realized how far into myself I had retreated, and how far distant I was from everyone else. Very likely, they were perplexed by my behavior, and, after a time, frightened. Their attempts to draw me back to them were not succeeding. Bubbeh, with her gentleness, and Daddy, with his awkward attempts to understand and console—neither of them could reach me. And yet at the same time, I needed these familiar people, these familiar angry tensions, even these familiar walls—they were the stuff of my life's experience. Our cramped flat was the center of everything that had meaning or memory for me. As much as I had longed to free myself from the hold of this place and its small community of unhappy souls, I would be bereft without them and stripped of the only bearings I knew. And, of course, the essence of Momma was in that apartment.

I needed rescue from remoteness and confusion, though rescue was hardly what I was seeking, for it would have separated me from my mother. But against what I thought were my wishes, it came.

It came in the form of one of the *landsleit*, or perhaps he was a cousin—to this day, I don't know which. Joe Astrove—born Yossel Asherovsky in a shtetl near Novaradugk—was the third of four brothers brought by their parents to the Lower East Side when still very young, around 1910. Though his formal schooling was brief, he had, after many struggles, done well as a manufacturer of children's snowsuits in the 1930s, at a time when such an article of clothing was a novel concept. The youngest of the brothers, Ralph, had found similar success after establishing a small plumbing and heating company, which continued to grow until it eventually achieved national stature. In their late thirties at the time of Momma's long illness, the two brothers shared a remarkable sense of obligation. They took it upon themselves to assume responsibility for members of their parents' far-flung network of old-world relatives and friends who might be in financial difficulties. As I would later learn, a series of checks in the amount of one hundred dollars each—a large sum in those days—had begun arriving in the mailbox of apartment A when Momma's condition reached the point where help was needed in paying the bills for her care.

Another thing I would later learn about was Daddy's resentment at having to take the Astroves' money. He saw it as a reflection on his ability to provide for his family's needs. But he had no choice, because without the help of Joe and Ralph, we could not have gotten by during those hard times, when financial problems had become even greater than they were under ordinary circumstances. The unacceptable had to be accepted, though it further shook Daddy's brittle pride, which had already suffered so many blows to its stability. Without the generosity of the two brothers, in fact, it would not have been possible to have had Esther with us in the weeks before Momma's death.

When Joe and his wife, Fanny, visited during shiva, they suggested that I spend a few days of the Christmas vacation period at their house in New Rochelle, a town about ten miles north of New York City, in moneyed Westchester County. At that time, New Rochelle was a prosperous community of tree-lined streets, a place imbued with the wholesome freshness I associated with an idealized suburbia. I was familiar with such picture-perfect small towns. I knew them from the many movies I had seen on Saturday afternoons at the Loew's Paradise on the Grand Concourse or at the more humble Oxford Theater on Jerome Avenue, under the shadow of the el.

As much as I longed for escape, the reality of it, for whatever the shortness of the period of separation, was a suddenly threatening intrusion into the fragile configuration of my world. Daddy was against it, believing it constituted yet another reflection on his fathering. But Bubbeh and Tante Aya had no such qualms. Both of them were fond of Joe and were convinced that only good would come of my being with him.

In the end, it was the power of Tante Aya's determination that wrestled me away from home and my thoughts. No objection by my father seemed strong enough to overcome her will. In their sorrow after Momma's death, she and Daddy had actually begun to speak to each other from time to time when it was necessary to address some mutual problem that Momma would have taken care of by herself. The tones in which they spoke on these occasions were so charged with obvious reluctance that their conversations always had an almost grudging sound about them. Tante Aya was a vigorous force, and not to be denied. She made their discussions about my leaving sound as though Daddy's reluctance was, in fact, selfishness. Within a few days, she had convinced me that a short time in the luxuriant surroundings of New Rochelle, spent in the company of Joe's twelve-year-old son, George, might be fraught with longing for home, but it would take place among people who cared about me. She also let me know her certainty that Daddy was thinking only about himself.

Ambivalence, uncertainty, the fear of my own wish to leave the circle of home—none of these worries left me, but I found something to reassure myself with and so ease my first foray into the Bronxless world: I would be going to a place where people had an understanding of my lingering reluctance and could be counted on to return me to my family on a few hours' notice should the separation be too much for me to handle.

On the appointed day, Tante Aya packed a few of my things into a tired old suitcase. Except for the time I had diphtheria, and an appendectomy when I was nine, this would be the first time I had ever been separated from my family. Driving her big shiny

Call: 1-800-693-8719 or go online: ConsumerReports.org/cr/new09 for your Consumer Reports New Car Price Report

Have your credit card ready and know the year, make, model, and exact model type of the vehicle you want to buy (see example below). Prices: $14 for the first Price Report; $12 for each additional report ordered at the same time. For Used Car Price Reports make sure to include the year, make, model, and trim line of the vehicle (e.g. 1995 Nissan Pathfinder XE 4-door 4WD). The cost for each Used Car Price Report is $12.

You now have three ways to order! Call the toll-free number above and your report can be mailed or faxed. Or, order online for instant online delivery. If you prefer to order your New Car Price Report by mail, just send this coupon with your check or money order in a stamped envelope to: Consumer Reports, P.O. Box 3900, Peoria, IL 61612.

EXAMPLE	2007	Honda	Accord	4-Door Sedan
[Please Print]	[Model Year]	[Make]	[Model]	[Exact Model Type]
1st Car				
2nd Car				
3rd Car				

Name _____   Phone Number (___) _____

Address _____

City _____   State ___   Zip ___

Price Reports on certain vehicles may not be available.

NCP07D

Buick (Daddy called this car a "Byutik"), Fanny came to pick me up in the late afternoon of December 28, and off I went, after tearfully kissing my tearful Bubbeh good-bye, while Daddy glowered with displeasure in the background. Bubbeh's last touch was to push my *chubikle* into place because it had, as usual, fallen forward onto my forehead.

George proved to be a friendly, good-natured boy, and he seemed genuinely pleased that I would be spending a few days sharing his room. And even better, he had a picture-pretty fourteen-year-old sister named Betty, whose vivacious presence added to my immediate impression that the spacious and beautifully decorated Astrove home was a Hollywood set come to life. I was bedazzled by everything I saw in it.

George and I were together constantly in the following days, tramping through the woods, walking on ice-covered ponds, playing games of every sort, and strolling like young royalty on a wide boulevard called—as though to fulfill my cinematic fantasies—Main Street. Together, we explored a world that was entirely new to me. My daily letters to 2314 Morris Avenue conveyed just a bit of homesickness, and at first my indecision about the day-to-day question of returning to the Bronx. But it would always be resolved by an eleven-year-old boy's wide-eyed delight with things he had never before encountered and was astonished to be enjoying. "I'm having too much fun to go home today" is a sentence I wrote on the fourth evening, encapsulating everything I felt.

If I turned inward toward Momma during that brief golden time, I have no recollection of it. I felt as though transported and transformed from all I had known, and comfortable to be in that distant place and among these good people. I never looked back on the solitary mourning I had so abruptly left behind. I would not have imagined such a thing could have come to be, and yet I never thought to wonder at it.

At last, the time came to leave the large sunny house in New

Rochelle and the new world I had discovered there. After almost a week in the glorious realm of the Astroves, I said good-bye to my new friend George and returned home. The undercurrent of homesickness had lessened with time, and I had stayed far longer than anyone might have anticipated. The kindly Joe had proven to be Judge Hardy, Squire Allworthy, and *Oliver Twist*'s Mr. Brownlow all rolled into one. Fanny, who was more reserved than Joe and possessed a sometimes lofty kindness, had seen to my welfare, my rudimentary table manners, and my other needs for gentrification. The world beyond the Bronx seemed no longer a terra incognita, much less forbidding, much more a manageable landscape in which I might find my way. I had touched it and even been a part of it for just a while. But I wondered whether I had merely been playing a role. Could Sherwin Bernard Nudelman of 2314 Morris Avenue, apartment A, I wondered, ever really belong in such a place as the one he had just seen?

I was given an opportunity to find out. One day about three months after my week in New Rochelle, a letter arrived from Joe—we had no phone in the house—asking whether he and Fanny might visit soon, because there was something they wanted to talk about with all of us. He gave no hint of what was on his mind. As I read it first to Tante Aya and then to my father, and later translated it for Bubbeh, none of us said a word of what we might have guessed was the purpose of the meeting. That evening, Tante Aya called the Astroves from the corner drugstore to invite them to come.

They arrived on the following Sunday afternoon, and the whole family assembled in the living room to hear what they had to say. After a few words of greeting, everyone chose a place to settle. Not realizing the significance of what he was doing, Joe set himself down in the large armchair in the corner, where Daddy always sat. It was the place that had been preempted by Uncle Manny on all those many evenings when he lingered with us after supper. Tante Aya sat in her usual corner location beyond the glass-doored bookcase that separated her cushioned seat from my father's customary place. Having no choice, Daddy took one of the folding chairs from their place behind the living room door and positioned it before the bookcase, so that he was sitting between Tante Aya and Joe, across the room from the couch, whose center cushion was occupied by Fanny. I took the place on her left and Bubbeh sat down at her right. Alongside me was Harvey, perched on the hassock he had moved from its place just in front of Joe. Not a word was spoken during all of the preliminaries of settling down. Everyone seemed ill at ease and tentative. There was an air of expectancy in the room, a sense of an apprehension that something was about to change, and not necessarily for the better.

Finally, Joe began. "You know," he said quietly, with the warm smile I had come to recognize for the goodness that brought it to his face, "when we need to make a big decision in our family, we all get together and have what we call a 'council.' Well, we did that last week—Fanny and Betty and George and I—and we talked about an idea I had. But it turned out that it wasn't just my idea. It was everybody's at the same time, and everybody agreed on it.

"Shep came to stay with us for a week and we all fell in love with him. He and George hit it off beautifully, and I know they're good friends now. Betty likes him very much—says it's like having another brother."

There was a brief pause. Joe's next sentence only confirmed what by then was the certainty in everyone's mind. "What Fanny and I came here to say is that we all want Shep to come live with us."

There was not a word of response from anyone in the room. I may have imagined it, but I thought I saw Daddy's jaw clench and unclench in the space of an instant, as though he had been jolted by the unexpected force of Joe's words and was struggling not to follow his immediate impulse to protest. Joe must have thought something would be said at that point, and he delayed for another moment before going on. But except for the abrupt disappearance of Tante Aya's smile, nothing changed in that eerily quiet room. Joe's face assumed its usual earnest expression and he continued on, starting again with the same words.

"You know, we've been very lucky in our family. My business has been good, we have a fine home in a lovely town, and there are so many advantages we can provide for our children. What we want is for Shep to come live with us so he can have some of the good things we've been able to give them. These are things you can't do for him."

Tante Aya started to say something but then stopped herself. Though Fanny's matronly form filled the space alongside me, I could see from the corner of my eye that Bubbeh had dropped her head after Joe's first few sentences and was staring down at her hands, folded one on top of the other in her lap. This meant that she was trying hard not to cry. Daddy, who remained motionless, was doing what he could to betray nothing, but the further visible tightening of his face gave away his attempts to hold himself in control. Joe, the soul of tact, as he always was, seemed not to notice, and he went on.

"I know how hard things have been here, and we want to help. Please think this over, and you'll see that we want only the best for Shep. And it will be good for our family, too."

This was the chance I was so sure I wanted, but now that it had actually been put forth, I was much less sure. I was desperate for Daddy to say yes, then and there. I wanted him to say yes so that I would not have to make a decision that moments ago had seemed so easy; I wanted him to decide for me so that the pangs of remorse I was already beginning to feel would be washed away by his enthusiastic acceptance of Joe's offer. When Joe began to speak, I had started to envision a joyous future, but his actual words had filled me with an unexpected dread. This was not the way it was supposed to be.

After another tension-filled pause, Daddy finally spoke. "Dis iss ah bick sooprice," he said, straining more than before to appear emotionless, though it was clear that he was thunderstruck by what he had heard. "I neffer tawt fin sotch ah tink. I dunt know vaht ta sayink."

He was more than surprised. I could tell, even if Joe still could not, that Daddy was deeply wounded by the proposal. I knew my father well enough to understand why, and yet I was unprepared for his response. No matter what was churning in his thoughts, he had somehow gathered the presence of mind to seem willing to think about what Joe had said. At least he did not reject the proposal in a spasm of insulted rage. It was unlike my father to hold back this way. It may have been in deference to the worldly success and therefore the legitimate authority he saw in Joe and the respect we all had for him. I had no idea why he was trying so hard to be restrained.

Tante Aya's response was different. She let her face relax before she spoke. "Ve vant only vot iss good fa Sheppy. It could be de best ting to go live vid you, Joe."

Fanny put her right arm around Bubbeh, who had understood not a word spoken in English but had grasped what was meant. Very gently, Fanny explained it all to her in the slightly uncomfortable Yiddish of a native speaker who rarely uses the language anymore. Bubbeh let her eyes fill with the tears she had until then been holding back, and she thanked Fanny and Joe for wanting to do such a wonderful thing. "What a future he could have if we did this," she said in Yiddish, smiling, though the tears did not stop. "But how could I get along without my Sheppy?"

I turned toward Harvey, but he said nothing. I knew that I had to make some kind of response, regardless of whether I addressed the issue. "I really had a good time in New Rochelle, and me and George got to be such good friends." I was repeating most of Joe's words, but I could not think of anything better to say. In my imagination, I was already there with the Astroves, looking forward a few years in time to my days at New Rochelle High School and all of those Betty-like girls, and in the meantime waiting for the bus every morning to take me off to the uncrowded classrooms and green playing fields of the nearby grammar school. George and I would have friends named Tommy and Jim, and we would play tennis—and baseball, on a real field with real bases—and I would wear saddle shoes and stylishly patterned sweaters all the time, like those I had seen on the robust torsos of teenage idols in the movies.

But where would I go to say Kaddish for Momma? And what about the kosher food I needed? I had given myself a temporary dispensation from these things during my week in New Rochelle, but not without pangs of conscience. Would the Tommys and Jims laugh at me for refusing to ride in a car or write on Saturdays? Could I visit 2314 Morris Avenue as much as I wanted to? And, finally, how could I do this to all of these people I needed so much? And what would happen to Harvey, who at that moment was act-ing as though he didn't care what I did?

But I wanted it, and I suppose I had wanted it since realizing how liberated and free I had felt at Joe and Fanny's house. I remem-bered my twinge—far more than a twinge, in fact—of reluctance while packing my suitcase to return home. This was the escape I had always been certain I would find, and it was coming to me in the form of a place and a family already known.

The offense that Daddy was obviously taking increased my resolve to accept their offer. Had he embraced Joe's overtures, I might have reacted in exactly the opposite way—maybe. But I was, at least during those moments, prepared to leave home. This was not the time to think of Fanny's reserve and her frequent critiques of my untutored table manners. Nor was it the time to think of my natural place in the midst of my own family; to understand my own life only in the context of being here in this very apartment, among the familiar and the beloved; to consider what life would be like for Bubbeh and for Harvey without me; or to acknowledge the guilt that was insistently whispering to me, as though I had already abandoned my family. Nor was it the time to remember that I belonged here with them, among the smells, the tears, the shouting, and the undercurrent of animosity, gloom, and old-world Jewishness. I didn't want to think about the scuffed brown shoes that perpetually needed soles, or the mended socks; the stickball and the Popeyes and Herbys and Dannys and Donnys; the smothering, constraining, and unthinkably bizarre form of unspoken love that I would never find anywhere but in that small apartment, among these peculiar people with their constant grumblings and conflict, their unhappiness, and their foreignness in this confusing land of America. This was not the time to remember that I shared their sense of looming tragedy, even if I did not yet understand that we kids were their consolation for everything they had endured.

This was not the time to think of any of those things. This was the time to think only of deliverance.

Daddy tried hard not to betray his thoughts. But I understood him well enough to know the severity of the wound he had sustained. I'll overcome it, I thought. And I can tell that Bubbeh and Tante Aya will realize that this is the best thing for me, once they get over their shock at the thought of my leaving them. As for Harvey—well, he has so many friends and so much going on in his life that he'll hardly notice that I'm gone. And anyway, there'll be less to put up with from someone he sees as a wise-mouthed kid brother who can be a pain in the ass in so many ways.

Daddy was the real reason I wanted to get away. It was unnatural to have a father like him, one whose moodiness and explosive temper were ever ready to change the atmosphere in the blink of an eye, and leave me cringing with alarm and even a sense of danger at what he might say or do. He was a constant source of embarrassment when we were in the street together. His hacked attempts at English, his increasingly obvious difficulties with walking, the eating habits that seemed to disgust me more with each passing year—all of them repelled me. Why couldn't he be like other men? Why couldn't I have a father who was like everyone else's? I was ashamed to be his son, and I wanted to be away from him. But I knew also that he was the greatest obstacle to my liberation, just as he was the greatest reason I wanted to leave.

By the time the two Astroves went home, they must have realized how deeply they had hurt Daddy. He was not able to maintain his ineffective pose of stony inscrutability on that afternoon any more than he had ever been, even in situations far less fraught with major consequences than this one. Body movements, a subtle change in his tone of voice, his refusal after the first sentences to look directly at Joe—all of it gave him away. When our two guests went somewhat uncomfortably to the door, he made a point of staying behind in the living room.

No sooner had they gone than he exploded in Yiddish and in English. "Who dey tink dey ah? Dey tink vot I kent tek kerr ahn mine un son? Dey tink vot I dunt know ha to be ah fahderr?" The fusillade was directed at no one in particular, though it was meant to be heard by all of us. He had been belittled, disparaged, treated like less than a father, even less than a man. He knew how to show them that he would not stand for it. There would be no further talk of my going to live with the Astroves.

The more violent his shouting became, the more Tante Aya argued in favor of Joe's proposal. The hurt she felt was only at the thought of my going away; her pride at the opportunity I had been given went beyond any consideration that Joe might be impugning her ability to care for me. Bubbeh, too, was convinced that my going to live with Joe could only be a good thing, though her pain at saying so—her words always directed at Tante Aya or one of us boys—was obvious.

No one asked Harvey what he thought, and he gave away nothing. He seemed forgotten in the uproar around him. As for me, I cried a little. Daddy's objections blew away my doubts, especially as his rantings began to contain an element of anger directed at me, as if I was in some way at fault—as if I had orchestrated Joe's offer and the discussion. He was behaving in precisely the way that convinced me I had to get away from him.

It was not to be. Daddy would not hear any further discussion of it. He would never forget the affront of that day. Though the beneficence and the guidance of Joe Astrove would follow me and ease my path until his death some thirty-five years later, my father never forgave him.

VII

So long as Momma still lived, Daddy was able to maintain a degree of intactness within himself. Momma had been the source of a kind of internal order, holding together the uncertain framework of his spirit. After she was gone, that order slowly faded in the same way that the immanence of Momma slowly faded from our everyday lives. When the reality of her was no longer present in the ordinary things we did, the reality of her was no longer present in the eroding foundation of my father. A part of him had been lost.

Tante Aya stepped forward after Momma's death and took the helm of our family as she had never before done. That change had been almost imperceptible over the course of the preceding months, but it became swift and sure after shiva was over. Despite taking the subway each morning into Manhattan and doing her laborious job at a garment-industry sewing machine, she somehow assumed responsibility for housekeeping, shopping, and most of the cooking, and she took charge of us two boys—and Bubbeh, too—as though she had been doing it all of our lives. She radiated authority. We began to call her Aunt Rose. Later, she would become simply Rose.

Aunt Rose was responsible for creating the atmosphere among us. It was her pace and her rhythm that determined the temper of our lives. She was a firm and even a tough presence, but a benevolent one nevertheless, who transparently pretended that she was caring for us only grudgingly. With chidings, unabashed appeals to our sense of obligation or even guilt, an occasional temperamental outburst, and ample displays of her tart-tongued humor, she never hesitated to make sure that Harvey and I knew exactly what was expected of us. I sometimes chafed under her suzerainty, but I loved her for the unspoken devotion with which she watched over us. Her brusqueness was easy to see through, and I loved her for that, too. Though I learned to get around her attempted aura of toughness by a kind of teasing banter sometimes, I feared her wrath when I let her down. As Bubbeh would so often say in the years to come, *"Zi firt de redel"* ("She controls the steering wheel").

Daddy had exerted much of his hegemony through Momma. She had been the calming intermediary between him and the strong-willed Lutsky women. It was Momma who had made it possible for him to go unchallenged in the household, or at least not be challenged directly. Now the channel for his forceful rule was gone. He seemed to recede, to become less significant.

Whatever Daddy still had of direction or control—all the frail stability of his wobbly gyroscope—began to falter. He gradually abandoned his pretenses of dominion; he drifted. As the years passed, being lost in America would give way to being lost in life.

Were Momma's death not enough, the process of my father's decline soon found yet another catalyst. It was as though destiny was determined to assure that there would be no interruption in the plans it had laid for him. There was to be no delay, and no relief.

It began a few months after Momma died, when my big brother was in his second week of working as a Saturday delivery boy in Krichevsky's fruit and vegetable market, Harry Rifkin's competitor on 183rd Street, around the corner from our house. A deluge of rain had been pouring down all day, and Harvey arrived home that evening in wet clothes and soaked shoes. A day or so later, he came down with a sore throat and fever. The sore throat lessened, but within a week he had developed pain and swelling in his wrists, elbows, and knees, and the elevation of temperature increased. As soon as Harvey pointed out the joint symptoms to her, Aunt Rose went to the corner drugstore and called Dr. Hochfeld, who was covering Willie's practice for the duration of the war. He came to the house as soon as his evening office hours were done.

Once again, we found ourselves gathered outside the closed door of my parents' bedroom, now being shared by Harvey and our father. And once again, the message was seen before it was heard. When the doctor finally came out of the room after a prolonged examination, his solemn expression prepared us for news that would not be good. Leo Hochfeld was a tall, balding man in his mid-thirties, whose soft-spoken gentleness belied the shattering effect of his opening sentence: "The boy has a heart murmur." *Murmur*—it was enough to terrify each one of us. The word *murmur* held connotations of serious disease, and to us, in our ignorance of such things, it meant disaster and perhaps death. How could vibrantly healthy Harvey be struck by the catastrophe that Dr. Hochfeld now told us was something called rheumatic fever? None of us had ever heard of such a sickness, appearing like a bolt of capricious fury from some unknown place. Daddy rumbled some harsh words about Louie Krichevsky for keeping Harvey out in such foul weather, but all he accomplished by the short burst of invective was to upset everyone at the thought of how easily this misfortune might have been avoided.

As Dr. Hochfeld proceeded to describe the usual course of rheumatic fever and the symptoms to watch for, we heard only one thing: the possibility of permanent damage to the heart. And then followed the ominous sound of something called "cardiac failure." At the very least, Harvey would be confined to bed for weeks or months, and then his activities would have to be restricted for a long time afterward—perhaps all his life. In what seemed an instant, he had been brought tumbling down from the heights of athleticism and youthful verve. We were being told that Harvey was a sick and potentially handicapped boy, possibly facing a lifetime of chronic invalidism. I was afraid to translate all of this to Bubbeh, but there was no choice. At the very least, the appearance of this new and unfamiliar sickness meant that yet another of her hopes, and the hopes of Daddy and Aunt Rose, had been shattered.

Harvey remained in bed for six weeks, during which time his only activity was an occasional walk to the bathroom, and even that was not permitted until almost a month had passed. Bubbeh took with utmost seriousness the doctor's recommendation that recovery would be hastened by hearty and fortifying nourishment—she plied Harvey with high-calorie food at mealtimes and milk-laced drinks in between. Chief among them was a classical Yiddish elixir known to all bubbehs everywhere as a *gawgel mawgel.* The fortifying effect of a *gawgel mawgel* was said to be so powerful that it was only to be called into action for situations beyond the capacity of the old standby, chicken soup. The concoction consisted of a large glass of milk laced with generous dollops of honey and butter, into which a raw egg had been vigorously stirred. When Harvey had sufficiently recovered to be allowed to shuffle into the living room on unstable legs for the first time, he had gained more than twenty pounds and was no longer the slim, gracefully coordinated fourteen-year-old boy he had been.

My current textbook of internal medicine, published in 1996, has this to say about patients who have recovered from the acute phase of rheumatic fever:

Once the acute attack has subsided completely, the patient's subsequent level of physical activity depends on cardiac status. Patients without residual heart disease may resume full and unrestricted activity. It is important that patients not be sub-

*jected to unwarranted invalidism, because of either their own
inaccurate perceptions of the nature of the rheumatic process or
those of parents, teachers, or employers.*

"Unwarranted invalidism" is an understatement for the restrictions to which Harvey was now subjected, despite being found to
have been left with no cardiac problems when the acute phase had
subsided—not even a residual murmur. The overcautious consultant
brought in by Dr. Hochfeld permitted no sports or other vigorous
activities, and he warned his young patient to do nothing more
strenuous than go to the movies. Harvey did not play ball again
until his twenties, and rarely even then. He became as sedentary as
a middle-aged accountant, continuing to gain weight during his
teen years, until he was more than forty pounds heavier than he
had been before his illness. His self-confidence waned, his buoyant
spirit was broken, and his enthusiasm, which had made him so
popular among his friends, vanished. Always an effortlessly good
student, he failed French at the end of the first semester after
his return to high school. He lost interest in his studies and there-
after got by with as little effort as possible. The Harvey I had
admired, envied, and ineptly tried to emulate in street games was
gone forever.

My father was devastated by his older boy's illness. He never
did understand it, except to know that in some way Harvey's heart
was affected and that he had been in danger of dying during the
early weeks. Very likely, the first few days of the illness resonated
in Daddy's thoughts, reminding him of the period of Maishele's
death and my diphtheria.

But this time, Daddy faced his fears alone. The one person in
whom he might have confided his uncertainties, his anxieties, even
his torment—with whom he might have shared them and perhaps
garnered strength—was lying in her grave.

It was a difficult six weeks for Daddy, but there was no moment worse than the one he endured on the evening when Dr. Hochfeld came out of the bedroom to tell us Harvey's diagnosis. In later years, he told me—here translated from the Yiddish—how he felt when he heard the stunning news:

"I went to a saloon on that evening when we were first told what was wrong with Harvey. I was miserable. All I wanted to do was to drink myself into oblivion. But when I got there, the place was so crowded that I stood for a long time just inside the door, too timid to push my way toward the bar. You know, Shepsel, I had never been in a saloon before, and I wasn't sure what to do in such a place. After about fifteen minutes of standing there, my head swimming with confusion and uncertainty, I opened the door and stepped out into the street. And then I went home."

I could not have imagined my father with his belly pressed against a bar, ordering a drink over the din of a crowded saloon—ordering a drink in his peculiar and sometimes indecipherable brand of English—those dark, pained eyes moist and glistening, the bowed and battered shoulders hunched in despondency. It would not have been Meyer Nudelman.

Daddy told me that he had focused all his store of optimism for Harvey's future on the outcome of a single hour, which came at the end of the six weeks of bed rest. It was then that the cardiology specialist came to the house for the final evaluation of his patient's condition and to make recommendations for the following months.

"As the weeks went by and Harvey seemed to be getting better, I began to put all my hopes in what that specialist would say," Daddy told me later. "A few days before he came, I made up my mind that if he gave me bad news, I would go up to the roof of some building and jump off. Bad news would have been the final calamity—nothing left after all these years except you and me—alone. And who knows where the next awful blow might come from? I couldn't bear any more of it."

And then, for some reason, Daddy stopped speaking in Yiddish and said in his fractured English, "I vud c'mi soozih."

I knew even as he said it that he was incapable of suicide. By then, I was a medical student and had enough understanding of my father to perceive that there was no loneliness or despair so great that it might overcome the almost perverse determination he had to persevere in spite of everything he had witnessed in his life. He might use the dreadful word, but he was incapable of the deed—not because of cowardice, although I did sometimes wonder about that possibility, but because of some unspoken and perhaps less-than-conscious conviction that he simply had to go on, not only then but always. The order of things demanded it. There was no choice.

And, of course, there was always some possibility of redemption at the end. Though I was in my twenties when my father told me this story, I somehow did not grasp even then that the redemption lay with his younger son—me.

And so my father soldiered on. In this, he shared more than he knew with Bubbeh and Aunt Rose. It was far too late for them to find their own happiness. It would be through the children that life would in time be found to have its greatest meaning, and its reward. They were able to endure because they lived their lives in the service of a dream.

Harvey's illness and the onset of his consequent long period of apathy added to the unraveling of the ill-knit fabric of my father's soul. Its fibers came loose in increasingly obvious ways. Although he became offended when Harvey or I tried to point it out to him, he was paying less attention to his appearance. His clothes bore ever more evidence of dropped food, and he rarely had them cleaned. He stopped retying his neckties each day, instead loosening them just enough for removal over his head and then a reverse of the process on a subsequent morning. In time, the knots became tightened into strangulated, wrinkled clumps, which overlooked a tie dotted with the ignored evidence of his unsteady hands laboriously bringing a spoon or fork to his mouth.

And his movements became more unsure. It was at this time that Daddy began increasingly to need me when the sidewalks were slippery. At first, this happened only when inches of snow had fallen or when the ground was treacherous with thin sheets of ice, but by the time I was well into adolescence, I had to walk with him even when conditions were much less hazardous. His grip on my arm became tighter as his sense of balance became looser.

One of the more unpleasant symptoms of Daddy's progressing spinal-cord disease soon began to make its odious—and odorous—appearance. He was losing the automatic and unthinking control of bladder function that most of us take for granted. This was the first sign of a disability that would plague him for the rest of his life. Now that the normal signals meant to indicate that he needed to urinate were absent, his bladder would at first occasionally and then more often become full without his knowledge, and a few drops of unnoticed urine would dribble into his underpants.

In the beginning, this was not much of a problem, but by the time I was in my midteens, it could no longer be ignored by any of us living in such close quarters. It was then that Daddy got into the habit of putting a small cloth into the front of his shorts so that the overflow could be absorbed. Ashamed to put the cloths in with the family laundry, he dried them in the fall and winter months by spreading them out on the radiator in his bedroom. Eventually, he had to do this so often that the room reeked of urine most of the time. When Harvey or I remonstrated with him, he responded with the predictable burst of insulted protest. After awhile, we stopped calling attention to the smell. As bad as it was for me, Harvey, who slept in the same room, bore the brunt of it. Fortunately, the bedroom door was always kept closed, and neither Bubbeh nor

Aunt Rose was confronted with the need to make any comment on the situation.

Worst of all was Daddy's obliviousness. He seemed not to be aware of his own steady slipping, perhaps because it proceeded at such a barely perceptible rate. I would often wonder if he noticed the stains on his clothes, or cared about the powerful smell in his bedroom. He had to have known of it, but he seemed to feel that there was nothing wrong with his way of dealing with the urine-drenched cloths. He took to using a stock phrase when one or the other of us would let slip a comment about it. "Ahm ah sick men" was his grumbling retort, and that was meant to explain everything, excuse it, and quash criticism or the request to do things differently.

It is almost too painful to think about, this self-recrimination I have borne since middle age about never having taken my father seriously. From very early in childhood, I had seen him as inept, unworldly, and ill-informed about everything. Volcanic in temper and terrifying in his autocratic control, he had always seemed to me to maintain his authority by the explosive force of his unpredictable and predictable anger rather than through any wisdom he possessed or respect he had earned. This was the intuitive sense I had about him, even as a child too young to put formed thought or words to it. Daddy's opinions and suggestions were not worthy of consideration because I was certain that he did not understand how the world works.

The ladies' garment industry being seasonal, Daddy was at home for long periods several times each year, uncertain what to do each day. He had no hobbies, saw friends rarely, and seemed a peripheral man in a household increasingly dominated by the personalities of its women and the needs of its boys. Reading the *Daily Forward* and other Jewish newspapers, venturing out on ever-shorter solitary walks as his mobility decreased, spending long hours at a candy store around the corner, whose proprietor welcomed his company—this is how he spent his days.

At some point during this time, both of us boys stopped calling him Daddy. He became Pop, as though in testimony to our increasing independence and his lessened—ever-lessened—hold over us. When Harvey and I spoke of him to each other in his absence, he was "your father," or "your old man," or sometimes "Meyer," a more marked form of estrangement, or even a disowning. More and more, he was a burden to us, and an embarrassment, too.

But at certain singular times, we did things as he wanted them done, because we realized—even as thoughtless and self-absorbed adolescents—there were moments that meant so much to him that we must accede to his needs. Among them were our annual visits to Momma's grave.

Jewish tradition ordains that the graves of loved ones be visited in the weeks before Yom Kippur, in order to ask that the spirit of the departed intercede with God on behalf of family and friends, so that a good year may be granted. And early each September, Pop, Harvey, and I made the pilgrimage, first going downtown to 145th Street on the Jerome Avenue el, then back uptown on another line, and finally getting onto a bus that crossed the Whitestone Bridge to complete the circuitous route from the Bronx to Queens and Mount Hebron Cemetery, where Momma was buried in the section allotted to the relatives of those belonging to the Workmen's Circle. A journey that would have taken twenty minutes by car consumed an hour and a half by public transportation.

We three would huddle together at Momma's grave, one son on either side of his father. The procedure was always the same during the approximately five years we followed it. With clumsy hands, Pop would pull from the side pocket of his coat a worn and remarkably unflattering photograph of Momma. Wordlessly, he then passed it to each of us in turn, so that we would remember what our mother looked like. But the Momma we knew barely resembled the round-faced, somewhat dumpy middle-aged woman in the picture, her hair combed in a drab, flat style—one we had seen only in the last few years of her life—and her dress a large one with transverse stripes. She looked ungainly and even squat. Each year, we looked at the same unattractive image of Momma, one we would rather not have seen. There could not have been a worse likeness. Why this particular one when there were others to choose from, photos that showed our mother in a better and more accurate light? We attributed Pop's choice to his bad judgment in all matters, and his inability to see things as they really were. It was yet one more burden to be borne, along with the rest of his disabilities. We looked at the photo with the gravity he expected, knowing that to him it was like saying a prayer of remembrance.

At the ceremony, we tacitly understood that Pop was to be treated with respect. We had no wish to add to his burdens. Certainly neither of us wanted to antagonize him in the midst of his thoughts at the graveside. Not only would it have been unjust and impious; it might have set off a towering rage, which would have violated the aura of that place, and Momma's memory. Though the potency of Pop's verbal assaults was diminishing as he himself diminished, he was still capable of volcanic responses to perceived insult.

Pop's tendency to see insult where none was intended was not confined to his relationships within the family. One of the more memorable examples of this sort of thing took place one afternoon when I was thirteen. The scene was a crowded subway car as I was accompanying Pop home from a hospital in the Bronx, where he had gone for a clinic (he called it "clinning") appointment. By that time, his bladder problems had become bothersome enough that he required periodic visits to urologists, and the public clinics were his only affordable means of care—especially then, with Willie doing his doctoring in the South Pacific. The clinics were cold and unfriendly places in those days, where patients were kept waiting for what seemed an eternity, sitting crowded together on wooden benches for at least an hour or more before being called by a self-important desk clerk to be seen by an even more self-important physician. "Nudelman!" the frozen-faced woman would shout into the corridor at the top of her cigarette-coarsened voice, as though expressing her contempt for the very sound of the name she was pronouncing. "Go into room three and take off your clothes." Like as not, the lordly physician would greet my fifty-two-year-old father—who always seemed so meek and small in those places, confronted by the authority of such powerful people—with some variant of "Back again, huh, Pop?" But "Pop" from the mouth of this condescending doctor was offensive. It meant old and infirm, and it meant doddering. Its intent was to demean. He had no right, this pompous ass. I bristled every time I heard the word, like an expletive, leave his smug lips. This was the Great Man's characteristic way of showing the accompanying intern how to speak with familiarity in the argot of the mass of unwashed unwell, who returned like mendicants again and again to this domain of patronizing medical infallibility.

Examinations were hasty, and meaningful conversations between doctor and patient did not exist in those harsh sanctums of imperious healing. Communication was limited to the very few words necessary to evaluate symptoms, carry out a limited but nevertheless jarring physical examination, and then quickly bestow some cursory advice and the inevitable scrawled prescription. Every person there was more aware than he had to be that this was charity care, delivered by self-congratulating medical icons summarily fulfilling the obligation of maintaining their staff appointments. A decade later, these men and their associates would become my model for how *not* to treat fellow human beings who need the help that only a doctor can give. In those unfeeling clock-driven places,

the only thing that approached kindness was an occasional patronizing remark. Condescension was disguised as caring, and any attempt
to retain dignity or even individuality was treated as an affront to the
hegemony of the doctors and nurses. Pride was checked at the door.
My father left his clinic appointments bruised in body and soul.

After one of those disheartening visits, we descended glumly
into the subway. We had waited such a long time for our 3:00 p.m.
appointment that the evening rush hour had already begun. I
helped Pop step over the small gap alongside the train platform
and enter the crowded subway car. I was seething with the injus-
tice of seeing my increasingly enfeebled father endure yet one
more demeaning clinic experience. He was tired, dispirited, and
only too aware of the buffeting that with every difficult year increasingly robbed him of his small remaining store of pride. At the next
stop, a trio of laughing and bantering young women about twenty
years old came aboard, and we found ourselves standing beside
them. Though pressed up against the doors, they seemed oblivious
to their surroundings, giggling loudly and shouting to one another
over the din of the rattling train. After awhile, the jocularity gave
way to an exuberance of clumsy jostling, and they were soon pushing one another heedlessly in every direction, as though no one
else was nearby. The train stopped at three or four stations, and I
could see by Pop's face that the noisy hilarity and his consequent
need to keep shifting position were becoming too much for him.
When the car swayed as it negotiated a wide curve, one of the girls
inadvertently backed into him for the third time. Pop was barely
able to maintain the precarious balance—both physical and mental—that he had achieved by an unsteady grip on the floor-to-
ceiling support pole near which he stood. I kept my eyes on him as
his ire heightened and the knuckles of both hands became white
with the effort of holding on. The girls never noticed his mounting
exasperation. To them, he was an inanimate object, an impedi-

ment to their enjoyment. It took only one more of their unthinking nudges before he erupted.

"Vod you tinkink you doink, you rotten goilss, vod you no goot," he shouted, and even the roar of the train could not drown the roar of the offended man at the end of the little bit of patience he possessed. "You pooshink me aron 'n hittink me lok Ahm ah nottink, lok Ahm nod eafen ah poysson. Stop ahreddy vid all di jompink 'n skrimmink 'n noyzes."

The response was predictable.

"Who the hell are you, old man? Go straight to hell."

And they laughed even more loudly than before.

"Vod you tuckink, gaw to hell? You tuckink lok diss to you fahder in you un howz? Who you tink you sayink to? You bonch bummerkehs, you!"

Pop's behavior, I was certain, must have appeared preposterous to every occupant of that speeding subway car. He was begging to be ridiculed.

Even these Irish-looking girls (at that time of my life, every threatening stranger appeared to be Irish) seemed to have figured out that "bummerkeh" meant floozie, and it made two of them laugh all the more. But the third one, a pug-nosed and suddenly mean-looking redhead, began swearing at Pop, and then imitating his mangled English in her shrill, nasal voice. He was beside himself, shaking with impotent rage and clenching the vertical pole as though trying to squeeze the life out of his tormentor.

With Pop's first outburst, all eyes in the overfull car had turned toward us. Many of the bystanders seemed amused by the maddened Jewish man unable to control himself, and the girls making fun of him. I felt entrapped in a vise of mortification, unable to respond to the horrible shrews on my father's behalf or to look directly at any of the people near us.

"Pop," I said as quietly as I could force the words through my clenched teeth. "Please. Please stop it, will you? People are laughing at you." I had chosen the worst possible words.

"Sharrop, you doop, you!" he retorted, and I was sure that everyone in the car heard it. "Doop" was one of the names he called me when he thought I was opposing him in something. I was used to it.

"But listen to me. Those stupid, jerky girls didn't even see that you were standing there." I knew better than to use the most inflammatory term in his lexicon, so I avoided pointing out that he was making a damn fool of himself. He was the one being the dope, not I.

I wanted to be anywhere but in that subway car; I wanted the time to be any time but that very moment. But Pop was so helpless against his rage that he could no longer form words. He sputtered something at me, then turned awkwardly to confront the hectoring young woman again, shifting his wide footing and his grip on the pole a few times in order to accomplish it. He must have looked absurd to everyone in the car. Whatever he was trying to say to his baiting antagonist was lost in the subway's roar. Just then, the train pulled into the Burnside Avenue station, and by some miracle, the three young women got off, laughing and tossing their Irish heads and their Irish asses. We had only one stop to go, but I stared at the floor during the entire minute or two of that remaining ordeal, afraid to aggravate my father by speaking to him, and embarrassed to look anywhere but down.

Pop must have mumbled "Meckink fin me ah demfool" and "Fa Kryseck" under his breath two or three more times between Burnside Avenue and the next station, at 183rd Street, which was our stop. He called me "doop" at least twice. When the train pulled into the station, he grabbed my arm for support, as he always did, and every bit of his outrage penetrated into the fierce grip he had on my skin. I barely felt it, because all I could think of was his public humiliation—and mine.

VIII

Employment in the ladies' garment industry during the middle of the twentieth century waxed and waned with changes in fashion or the seasons. Several times each year, there would be weeks or more than a month of layoff for either Rose or my father, a slack period, which in my daddy's terminology was called "di sleck tseason." During those difficult times, we lived solely on one salary—our only other means of support the federal unemployment compensation of twenty-five dollars a week. In order to register for benefits, Pop had to trudge many blocks each Thursday, then stand on a long, slow line in the large, always crowded office he called "di onnemployink." Then, having finally reached the head of the queue, he would be confronted by an aloof clerk and required to scrawl his almost illegible signature onto a blank space at the bottom of a complex government form that he could not read. This signature was the only English script he ever learned to write.

Most of the time, Pop would have to manage the fatiguing journey on his own, because Harvey and I were at school. He somehow accomplished it even when the sidewalks were not completely free of ice or snow, usually by hesitantly asking strangers to help him negotiate slippery stretches of pavement as he came to them. With the passing years, the need for assistance became more and more frequent, and the expeditions to the unemployment office stretched themselves out into undertakings that lasted an entire morning or afternoon. I would accompany him on the few school holidays when I was at home, but I groused so much about losing the hours with my friends that he would sometimes plod off alone even when I could have gone with him. When the pavements were particularly treacherous, I could find no excuse not to make the arduous journey, so I had the opportunity—if it can be called that—to make my first observations of the federal bureaucracy.

The inefficiency was so rampant that it seemed to be almost deliberate. The clerks' petty importance was magnified by a certain sadistic pleasure they got from their dominion over the mostly Italian and Jewish immigrant workers who depended on their approval in order to get a weekly check without interruption. The prevailing mood in that teeming place of multiple maddeningly slow lines was one of irritated determination to make things difficult for men and women who had no choice but to do as they were told. It was not uncommon to see some poor fellow who had reached the clerk's counter after a protracted period of shuffling forward bit by bit being told that he was on the wrong line or had come on the wrong day, or that some minor irregularity on his form prevented its completion until it was sent back to a regional facility for reprocessing. Only rarely did a petitioner have the temerity to raise his voice or in any other way show displeasure over the treatment he was receiving. Those occasions would prompt the summoning of a supervisor, often emblazoned with suspenders and a large mustache. Conferring on himself all the authority of the United States government, he would inform the troublemaker that he must leave the facility and return when he could show more respect for the proceedings of its officials.

In that atmosphere of official disdain, a communal air of meekness prevailed among the unemployed workers, and it always made me angry. Like all the others in the congested room, I had no way of expressing my exasperation, but I could at least be sullen, and resentful of my father for needing to be there—and, in turn, for having the sort of physical disability that necessitated my presence there with him. It was yet another example, I was sure, of Pop's taking advantage of being "ah sick men" in order to take advantage of me.

Most of the time, Aunt Rose's slack season would overlap Pop's for only a short period. When it did, though, the contrast between the way the two of them handled their leisure hours was striking. She made use of them to clean the apartment with a thoroughness impossible at other times, rearrange furniture, complete small repairs and odd jobs around the apartment that had needed doing for some time, mend clothes, shop, visit friends, and be involved in a multitude of other bustling activities that kept her on the go all day long. Meyer's days in our confining apartment, on the other hand, were long and monotonous.

Pop's December "sleck tseason" usually coincided with my extended Christmas–New Year's break, as it did during my sophomore year in high school. On one of those dull, boring afternoons, Pop suggested that we go to the movies together. He had little interest in movies, so the time must have been passing with particular tedium or he would not have wanted to do such an unaccustomed thing, especially since the effort of getting to the theater on a cold, windy day in late December was considerable. I dragged my heels about deciding whether to go, reluctant as always when I had to take him to a place where I would rather not be.

He gradually won me over by his repeated urgings, telling me again and again how it would relieve the dreariness of that endless series of bleak winter days if he could only get out of the house for a few hours. Snow had piled up on the curbs and in the gutters during the several weeks of his enforced idleness. He had left the house just a few times, and then only briefly. Even a fourteen-year-old boy as self-absorbed as his younger son could not help feeling sorry for him.

I, too, rarely went to the movies. I had gotten out of the habit of the weekly Saturday-afternoon hegira to the fifteen-cent double feature (plus newsreel, plus cartoon, plus sports reel, plus chapter in an adventure series) in the year after Momma's death, when Jewish mourning customs prohibited entertainment of any sort, and I had never resumed going. Though having begun a series of after-school and vacation jobs the spring and summer I was eleven (I was a delivery boy for Harry Rifkin, a shipping clerk in a men's shop on Fifth Avenue, and I also picked up a few extra dollars by baby-sitting at a quarter an hour), I had to spend my income on clothes and other personal necessities, so I was chronically short of money. Any lingering doubts that I had about going to a movie were dispelled when Pop said that he would pay for the tickets. For him to make such an offer at any time, and especially in his present unemployed state, was evidence of his desperate need to get out of the house. We had no television in 1945, the Yankees didn't play baseball in the winter, and none of my friends had answered when I yelled up at their windows, so I thought I might enjoy a few hours' respite from boredom.

The closest—and cheapest—movie house was the Oxford, on Jerome Avenue just south of 183rd Street, which specialized in third- (maybe fourth- or fifth-) run adventure and romance films. Pop was keen to go, even though neither of us knew what was playing or when the show started, and the *Daily News* did not carry local listings. But getting there bundled up against the cold would be a more difficult undertaking than usual. In addition to the frozen patches on the pavement, the streets had been made even more treacherous because of a snowfall of several inches two days before. With Pop fearful of each step and holding fast to my right arm, it took us some thirty minutes to negotiate the four blocks to the movie house. We had to stop several times on the way because the effort of each step was so great that he quickly became fatigued. In addition to that, our expedition was made more hazardous by his overcaution, which contributed to a few near falls in which he almost brought me down with him—a performance I now realize I was better at preventing literally than figuratively.

At last we stood on the final street corner, with the theater's marquee in plain view. I looked up, momentarily ignoring Pop's pre-occupation with the slippery footing, and was chagrined to discover that the movie was one of the very few that I had already seen.

"Sorry, Pop, but I saw this movie a few weeks ago at the RKO Fordham."

"So? So you see ahgenn."

"No, I won't."

"Vod you say, vun't? Vod you say me, vun't? Ve go, noh? It juss cruss di strit. Unly heff ah block."

And then, with the adamant negativity of a stubborn adolescent determined just this once to be free of his father's insistent dependency, I said, "I'm not going, and that's all there is to it. Pop, let's go home."

He could not believe I meant it. Taking a badly balanced step in the direction of the theater, he almost fell backward because the unyielding young arm to which he was holding so fast would not budge.

"Pliz, Sheppy, I eskink you pliz. So fah we cummink and voz fa me hodt. Pliz dun't be lak det."

"Well, it's too bad," I said. "C'mon, let's turn around."

How unfeeling could I have been that my answer was so curt? Turning around would be complicated and awkward, because Pop could only do it by picking up his feet and replanting them in a slightly different direction in the poorly shoveled snow. He would have to do this several times, without letting go of my arm, as I moved bit by bit with him. This would require that we succeed in a clumsy series of maneuvers choreographed independently by its two struggling participants, trying hard not to tumble into each other. As practiced as we were at such a complicated process, we had never become very good at it.

He began to plead with me like a small boy, his voice finally breaking with what must have been the heartaching frustration of my refusal and the frigid resolve that gave rise to it.

"Ha could mine un son do me dis? All di vay fa nuttink, you'n me? I vonna gaw to di mooviss; dun't meck me I should gunk beck. Sheppy, I not gunk beck. Sheppy, I beggink you, pliz, pliz. It's fa me hodt. I ken't do det vaht ve gunk beck. Ahm ah sick men."

And then in Yiddish, he added, *"Shepsel, hob rakhmones"* ("Shep, have mercy").

None of it was to any avail. I had heard it all—particularly the "Ahm ah sick men," which I scorned as the ultimate evidence of inadequacy, a gambit to be pulled out when all else failed—too many times before, and my immunity had grown with the years.

This was one of the few times my father had not become angry when crossed. When such an unusual thing happened, his usual impotent rage was merely impotence. And though I refused to admit it to myself, he was piteous, standing there, a shell of a man—even more than usual—and imploring a steely willed, chronically contemptuous fourteen-year-old. A few hours' respite from the drear and loneliness of his cheerless life were all that Pop was asking for, and I was denying him even this small pittance of relief. Anyone with an iota of compassion would have responded to the anguished emotion in those moist deep brown eyes, but not Meyer's own son. His own son was beyond being moved. Pop's pleadings only hardened my heart. I treated them with disdain.

He was confused and hurt that I could be this obdurate when his need was so great, and within a few moments he was near tears. But no matter what he said, and regardless of the plaintive strain in his voice, my stupefying adamancy only worsened.

I look back on the unthinking cruelty of my behavior that day with some perception of its inevitability, or at least its justification in the perpetrator's mind. But at the moment, I was thinking only of what an embarrassment my father was being to me. Passersby were beginning to stare at us, and my only wish was to get away from the mortifying image we were presenting for all to see.

Finally, Pop gave up. Resigned, he consented to be taken back home—dejected, wearied, and alone with his thoughts. The entire distance was uphill, and the return was even more difficult than the trek outward. It took us more than forty-five minutes to make our silent way back to 2314 Morris Avenue, with him staring watchfully and worriedly at the pavement all the way there. I thought he would weep when he finally collapsed onto a kitchen chair before even removing his hat and his ill-fitting overcoat, but I did not care. Without saying a word, I left the apartment in a hurry, hoping to find one of my friends on the next block.

The images described and the events I have thus far recounted are among those many that have never left my store of memories. But I remember or have recalled more trifling moments, too. Had I been unable to retrieve them, it would not have affected my chronicle. They are the trivia of a life, but, however inconsequential, they refuse to remain forgotten in the cluttered storage places of my mind.

And so when—as in what follows—I cannot accurately bring forth some component of one particular experience that I believe to have had real consequences, I struggle to find an explanation. It is a commonplace that painful memories are likely to be repressed, and yet so many of mine are accessible nevertheless. Why not this one? How is it that I remember so much, but in this single instance remember not enough? Why do even insignificances appear to me unbidden, while this glaring gap remains?

I can remember most of the episode I am about to relate as

though it happened an hour ago, but what I cannot reconstruct is the moment that led up to it.

Late one February evening when I was fifteen, my father and I played out particularly memorable roles in a scene of the drama in which we were, until his death, cast together.

I have thus far described the events of our intertwined lives as though I had by the age of fourteen developed a lofty immunity to my father's displeasures and rancors. In fact, that was hardly the case: The immunity was only partial, and inconsistent at best. In spite of every loss to fortune's determined campaign against him, Pop, when provoked, could still inflict on me the unique form of fear and trembling that remained from my childhood memories of him. Perhaps because Rose's hegemony over our family's atmosphere and rhythm had become so firmly established by my mid-teens, he rarely—except in the form of grumbling—expressed the unrestrained ire that had come so easily to him in the past.

I do know that my father's anger that evening was over something I said to him while we were standing in apartment A's front bedroom, which I was sharing with Bubbeh and Aunt Rose at the time. Whatever were my long-forgotten and elusive words, I can only remember the sensation that I meant them merely as a bantering remark about whatever it was that we were discussing.

No sooner were the now-forgotten offending words out of my mouth than, all at once and without an iota of warning, my father let loose a startling detonation of shouted abuse that exploded in my face so unexpectedly that I took an inadvertent step backward. I just stood there, shocked into frightened incomprehension, as I was subjected to a stream of castigation. I was unnerved by it, momentarily staggered, flummoxed by my utter inability to find justification for the massive retaliation, to the point of being able only to stand there paralyzed, unable to defend myself against its ferocity. I had hit some very sensitive chord, but I had no way of knowing what it was.

Meyer was infuriated and livid, consumed in that eruptive instant by a white-hot rage. It had ignited, flared, and blazed up into an out-of-control conflagration of fury immediately on the instigating words having reached his ear. In spite of years—decades— of trying to retrieve those words or the subject to which they pertained, I am no closer to knowing what they were than I was at the beginning of my search.

As always, he was seeing derision where none was intended. His fulminating response was as though all the frustration and stifled grievances of the years since Momma's death had in that microsecond found an outlet. I was at that moment the focus of everything he had endured.

The suddenness and ferocity of this hellish inferno of instantaneously discharged emotion exceeded anything I was prepared for or had ever experienced. Thundered words and accusations tumbled out of my father's mouth in a torrent of roaring sound so fast, so loud, and so confusingly jumbled that I barely understood them. But there was one thing I did understand: This deeply flawed man who inevitably felt himself degraded was now degrading me.

In an instant, I was reduced to childlike terror. I distorted my features in pain before the onslaught; I slammed both hands firmly over my ears to shut out the sound; I pressed my eyes as tightly closed as I could to shut out the sight. But nothing could shut out my father. Here was Meyer Nudelman, suddenly back in all his capricious power, all his paroxysmal menace. He would have his retribution. I cowered before him. I cowered physically, and emotionally, too, my self-confidence completely shaken.

My defenselessness itself added fuel to the fire of his wrath. I was powerless with fright, shrunken by it, made puny. I stood the vilifying as long as I could, and then, blubbering uncontrollably, rushed beyond the reach of his gesticulating arms and out of the room. Running for refuge into the living room, I pushed past Bubbeh and Rose, who stood in the hallway in disbelief at what they were witnessing. As I ran forward to throw myself facedown on the couch, the last thing I saw clearly were the alarmed looks in their eyes.

Like a man possessed and run amok, Pop stumbled after me as fast as his uncertain gait would allow. Though I buried my tear- and snot-soaked face deeply into the overstuffed cushion of the couch and curled up my body in a position of defensiveness, there was no escaping him. In a frenzy now, he stood over me, raving imprecations. In his most outraged moments, he had never dispar- aged me as he did in the enormity of the tirade he was now unleashing. The piercing showers of unbearable invective being flung down at my body were almost palpable. Insults one upon the other were hurled at me—debasing insults, propelled forth in that confused jumble of Yiddish and English that Meyer Nudelman fell into when he lost command of himself.

My own father was my tormentor, towering over me with waving arms, roaring his denunciations. Even knowing that my words were muffled by the cushion and choked by my racking sobs and the gurgling of mucoid wetness bubbling out of my nose and mouth, I kept begging him to go away. I was being suffocated by the savagery of his castigation. My head ached from the unre- lenting pressure of the words, which I could almost feel. Com- pletely beyond control now, he was flaying the skin from my soul.

I had no way of telling what Bubbeh and Aunt Rose were doing during those few excruciating minutes. I knew only that the bombardment of maniacal fury was doing its work, reducing me to a terrified and helpless infancy, and there was no way to protect myself against it. I was being paid back not just for my moment of mild teasing, but for all the indignities of a failed life as well.

And then, just as suddenly as it had started, the eruption stopped. Perhaps exhausted by his outpouring of violent energy, my father fell silent, and I sensed that he was motionless, too. Not daring to raise my head, I listened as he stomped away into his bed-room. He slammed the door behind him with so much force that I thought I could feel the couch shudder beneath me. I lay there for at least ten minutes, unable to believe it was over and incapable of stopping my hysterical weeping. Even Bubbeh sitting down on the edge of the couch and softly stroking my head did not help. Rose's response to the emotional carnage was to shout her loathing of my father at the closed bedroom door. He had to have heard every word she said, but he never appeared until the next morning, when he stormed out of the apartment without breakfast to go off to work.

Finally, I was able to get enough control of myself to sit up on the couch and let Bubbeh try to soothe my whimpering. Rose thudded out of the room, and her heavy steps were like a sequence of determined drumbeats on the bare wood floor. She sat by herself in the dark kitchen for a long time, and was still there twenty minutes later when I got into bed and tried unsuccessfully to sleep. When she came into the room after about an hour, it was only to say a few contemptuous words about my father before returning to the kitchen. Her disdain for him made me feel just a bit better about myself, and I soon fell asleep.

I thought it was all over the following day. When my father came home from work, he acted as though nothing had happened. I had long been accustomed to this pattern: He would explode into one of his excesses of rage and then within hours or a day appear to have forgotten all about it. It seems that he never believed there were any lasting effects from his thunderstorms of emotion.

But Bubbeh and Aunt Rose were staunch believers in the importance of holding on to a grudge; when the boiling stopped, the quiet simmer was encouraged to persist for a lifetime. Their own fractious relationship and the enduring fragility of their truce was the result of numerous barely resolved mother-daughter clashes that must have begun in Novaradugk. But they lived in harmony, despite this low level of friction. It was nothing compared to the ongoing animosity they nurtured against Meyer for some long-ago offense, whose nature I would never discover. Every one of his outbursts was like a booster shot to the acute antipathy that expressed itself as ill-disguised contempt. After Momma's death, he and Aunt Rose had declared an armistice in the interest of us two boys, but it was at first more like a prolonged cease-fire than a real peace. They spoke to each other—in the early years, they discussed only essential family matters, but later they talked more easily about ordinary things—but I always sensed that a small flare-up could occur at any time, and it not infrequently did. I knew that my father admired all that Rose was doing for the household, and especially for Harvey and me, and that he was sincerely grateful to her for holding all of us together in a real home. But I also knew that her attitude toward him was one of toleration. They lived in the same apartment, but the beloved intermediary was gone. There was no choice but to get along.

Rose could not easily allow my father's actions on that awful night to leave the forefront of her mind or to cease affecting her attitude toward him. The atmosphere of high tension in the apartment did not let up for weeks after. She barely spoke to him during all that time, and her few words were brief, brusque, and confined to only what was absolutely necessary.

I had the enthusiasms of school and my friends to distract me. Slowly, I let the events of that night recede from my mind. The process was no doubt made easier by my having been subjected to so many exhibitions of my father's mercurial temper in years past, but, whatever the reason, within a few days I was back to my usual active adolescent pursuit of everyday matters.

Having for the most part outgrown the street games of Popeye's Gang, I had in those teen years a circle of six or eight friends with whom I hung out. Though much of our wide-ranging discussions concerned major-league baseball (I bought myself a fifty-cent slide rule so that I could calculate batting averages, and to this day, I can use it only to divide), we spoke also of books we were reading, school, and of our mutual fascination with natural science. Since the age of twelve, we had all been studious keepers of tropical fish, periodically traveling by subway to the tip of Manhattan, where a huge commercial aquarium supplied all our needs at cut-rate prices. There was much to discuss about the care and breeding of the fish, which inevitably encouraged our mutually burgeoning interests in biology.

And, of course, we talked about girls. All of us went either to De Witt Clinton High School or the Bronx High School of Science, the latter conveniently located in an old building on the block adjacent to 2314 Morris Avenue. Neither school was coeducational, and that was also true of Creston Junior High School, on 181st Street, where our friendship had coalesced. The consequence of the female-barren years was that we knew few girls, and those only from a distance or superficially. But that never prevented us from being fascinated by females, especially in the sexual sense. Our very deprivation made the urgency greater than it might otherwise have been. We spoke often of our individual fantasies or of the possibility of laying this or that older woman.

These were the days of pimples and secret masturbation (which we believed to be effect and cause), of the fevered excitement of reading about sexual matters in tabloid reports of divorces and violent crimes, and of seeking out what we called the "hot parts" of novels. Harvey kept a copy of *Studs Lonigan* in a drawer, hidden under the velvet bag containing his prayer shawl and phylacteries, and I, without his knowledge, would read and reread some of the pages, which at that time seemed so salacious.

The intensity of my urges, the chronic state of sexual frustration, and my interest in tropical fish came together in a remarkable way one afternoon when I was attracted by the blond pageboy tresses of a blowzy young saleswoman in the pet department of the W. T. Grant department store near the corner of Fordham Road and Morris Avenue. She became for a time the fantasized object of my one sexual activity, which was jerking off behind the locked bathroom door. Intent on the impossible dream of possessing her for real, I schemed to come as close to that imagined ecstasy as I could. On busy afternoons at Grant's, I would step up behind her in the congested aisle of fish tanks and pass my hand as though by accident across her buttocks as I casually walked by. It was a technique I had mastered during many rush hours in the crowded subway as I went to and from my Saturday job as a shipping boy at Finchley's, a men's store on Fifth Avenue at Forty-sixth Street. Not deterred by being unable to feel very much through her girdle—an article of clothing that all women wore in those days—I returned again and again to my pubescent and literally underhanded bit of (again, literally) legerdemain. I must have brushed my hand across that much lusted-after ass eight or ten times in the course of the first month alone, but the hot blonde never seemed to notice.

When I was thirteen, fourteen, and fifteen I used to worry about the intensity of my sex drive. Sometimes after becoming aroused by reading a particularly lurid story of violence against a woman—always on page 4 of the *Daily News*—I would brood about what I was certain was the very real danger that I might in time become either a sex fiend (though I wasn't completely sure of what that term meant) or a rapist.

Two weeks after the terrible incident with my father, three of us—Ronnie Chapnick, Tommy Pappas, and I—took the subway downtown to Madison Square Garden and bought upper balcony seats to the AAU track championships. It was a wonderfully colorful event, far more exciting than the high school meets we were accustomed to seeing, and we left the Garden elated from the evening's fun. On going down into the subway, we found ourselves in the midst of a cheerful crowd of people who had exited the arena with us. The car we entered was quickly filled with the noisy exuberance so characteristic of large groups of sports fans who have just shared the enjoyment of an exhilarating athletic event. We found ourselves near the center door of the car, all three of us chattering away and feeling good just to be in such a convivial atmosphere.

When the train reached the Fifty-ninth Street station, three young black men entered, who instantly—and no doubt intentionally—caught the attention of everyone present as they delicately but firmly pushed their way toward the end of the car without interrupting a conversation they had begun on the platform. Having reached their carefully chosen destination, they turned themselves so that they faced the rest of the passengers and could be easily seen by anyone who cared to look, which they must have known would include everyone. They were apparitions of femininity. Each of them wore rouge, mascara, and face powder, and their straightened hair was done in a variety of elaborate salon styles, so carefully coiffed that every strand was in its precise place. The movements of their hands and arms were exaggeratedly female, and their dark Maybellined eyes flashed with the spirited abandon of their conversation. Conspicuously acting as though unaware that anyone else was present, they were like a gaggling trio of young actresses who had just stepped out of a cosmetics commercial. Except for their clothes, which were exquisitely tailored, there was nothing male about them.

I could not stop looking at the spectacle the three young men had created on entering the car. It took about ten minutes for the train to reach the 125th Street station, where they got off, by which time most of the passengers had resumed talking in their own small groups.

But not I. I was intensely troubled by what I saw. Even after they left the train, I kept thinking—brooding, in fact—about them. Ron and Tommy tried to engage me in conversation, but I would not be distracted from my ruminations.

It had only been a few months since I had discovered the existence of homosexuality, and here it was, staring me in the face in the form of three effeminate young men. I could not escape the crawling sensation that there was something about their blackness and the wenchy seductiveness they affected that made me feel threatened.

My brief introduction to the subject of homosexuality had occurred during one of the many bull sessions that passed for philosophizing among my coworkers in Finchley's shipping room. Holding forth that afternoon was a perpetually dour, sallow-skinned fellow named Ernie Gorman, who was called "the Flash" because of his dazzling speed with cardboard boxes, twine, and shipping labels. Ernie was a middle-aged bachelor who lived in Hell's Kitchen with his married sister's family, and I had long suspected that the reason he pontificated so much in our basement head-quarters was that no one listened to him at home. I usually ignored his Tenth Avenue pretensions of worldliness, but on this day he was speaking about something I had not previously heard of: He had just referred to a young man in the tailoring department as a "fairy" and a moment later as a "queer," and I asked him to tell me what he meant. His reply came in the thick New Yorkese that was the standard dialect of that place.

"Dey're boys what like to fuck udder boys."

"What do you mean? That doesn't make any sense."

"Da hell it don't. Dey stick deir prick in udder guys's assholes. Ya stoopid aw sump'n, kid?"

It was a repulsive thought, and I didn't understand it. "But why would they do a thing like that?" I asked. And then an idea flashed into my mind, though it seemed impossible to imagine. "You mean they feel about men the way we feel about women?"

The Flash must have thought I was spoofing him. After all,

how was it possible, in the world he knew, to reach the age of fifteen and not have come across fairies and queers?

"Yeh, dat's just wod I mean. Ha come ya didn't know wod id is, huh? Ya pal Buddy's one, ya know. Ain't he tried to do it to ya yet? Don't worry, kid, he will. Ya could be sure a dat."

I was stunned that such a thing could be. Buddy Rappaport, assistant to Mr. Carlo, the fitter, lived one station stop from me, and for months we had traveled home together on every one of my working days. From time to time, he and I had spent our lunch hour visiting his soft-spoken friend Neil, who worked a concession stand at the Booth Theater on Forty-sixth Street. Buddy's face was heavily powdered, he always smelled slightly of cologne, and his hair was dyed a blond-brown not found in nature, but I had assumed that he was simply sissified. That was to be expected, I thought, in a fellow only five-foot-three—which was also my explanation for his not having been drafted at a time when virtually every able-bodied man in his twenties was in the service.

Though now informed by the Flash, I never spoke to Buddy about these revelations. We kept taking the train together, and our usual small talk did not change, but I could not help imagining him at his perversions. And his friendship with Neil was now also to be seen in a suddenly new and harsh light. Buddy never said a suggestive word to me, though, even forewarned, I might not have recognized it if he had. With all the intensity of my sexual cravings for women's bodies, it was inconceivable that anyone, even my effeminate pal Buddy, could feel precisely the same way about men.

But that evening a few months later, in the subway car with those three boy-girls, I felt an inner fear. Was it possible, I found myself wondering, that I could be a fairy and not know it? Once it appeared, the tormenting notion refused to leave my mind.

In subsequent days, I became consumed with worry that I might be like one of those boys on the subway car, despite feeling no attraction toward men. I began to examine my thoughts, my urges—even the way I walked and my appearance in the mirror—looking for any sign that I might have previously missed. Determined to prove to that inner questioning voice that I was the epitome of masculinity and no fairy or queer, I found myself thinking of little else.

Obsessed with the entire spectrum of maleness and power, I remembered a fistfight I had backed away from when I was twelve, with a flinty, tough kid I hardly knew. I had had my share of punching or wrestling scraps of the sort boys get into, but they had always been with opponents from my own circle, and so the danger had been limited. But this fellow had been something else, a loner, someone who seemed not to have any friends. He lived with his tall, gangly janitor uncle in a basement flat on Walton Avenue, and there was something about the two of them that bespoke Jukes and Kallikaks. He would walk the streets by himself, seeming to slink along the curb, deep in discontented thought; sometimes there was a sly smile on his face, as though he had a secret. I never saw him in school and I never knew his name. One afternoon, we got into a squabble over something—I no longer remember what—and he wanted to fight. I was afraid, and did not take up the challenge. I walked away feeling like a coward, and from time to time after that day, I would torture myself with the recollection of it. I would keep telling myself that the slate could be wiped clean by my finding that boy and beating him up, but I somehow knew that I never would.

In the worst moments of my self-degrading preoccupations, I thought of myself as a coward and a fairy—no man, in any event. I felt I did not deserve the sexual fulfillment about which I had fantasized so much, and I certainly did not deserve marriage or worldly success—these were only for real men, and I was anything but a real man. I had shown it by refusing to fight that day, and this was now of a piece with my growing fears that I also might be a homosexual.

The obsessive preoccupation with all of this led rapidly to a kind of constant introverted sadness. Prior to those days, it was unknown for me to be unhappy for more than a brief time. Under ordinary circumstances, I was usually filled with energy and motivated by a multitude of enthusiasms. But now, all I could think about was the specter of cowardice and homosexuality. I became so depressed that I had trouble eating. Bubbeh made me custards, Jell-O, cereal, and other simple fare, but I turned away most of it. The family watched in deepening helpless despair as I became further detached from them, always morbidly sad and deeply focused on my fearful thoughts of inadequacy. My father did not know what to make of my descent into a despondency he had never seen, and, having nothing else to offer, he became touchingly gentle with me. But as always, he could not help but be clumsy in his gentleness, and it made us both feel awkward. Rose was convinced that the entire problem was due directly to what he had done to me less than three weeks before the first evidences of my withdrawal into myself. She did not hesitate to tell me so.

I decided to see Willie and tell him everything I was worried about, certain that, with his all-knowing ways, he could help me. His solution was to counsel me that such thoughts were not abnormal at my age and that they would go away. But instead, matters only continued to get worse. After about a week of this, he recommended that I see a psychiatrist, and said he would pay the fifteen-dollar fee.

Accompanying me to a psychiatrist was deemed too formidable an undertaking for Pop or even Aunt Rose, and in any event, it would have meant a day's lost wages. Harvey, who was a college freshman at NYU's business school, took time off from classes to go with me to the office of Dr. Moses Jacques Madonick, which was located on the Grand Concourse, near 167th Street. There was an air of gentle wisdom about Dr. Madonick, and he understood me. After confirming what Willie had said, he suggested that though recovery would be spontaneous, it might be facilitated if I took a cold shower every day and then vigorously dried my body with a thick Turkish towel until my skin was a glowing pink. It seemed a manly thing to do, and I thought of it as a vote of confidence.

Just speaking with Dr. Madonick and listening to his calm and assured voice made me feel better; my improvement began during the hour I was with him. Even after I was completely well, which took about three weeks, I continued to take a cold shower every morning and to rub myself pink. Since my Bar Mitzvah, I had been putting on prayer shawl and phylacteries to recite the morning service at the living-room table each day before breakfast. Concerned that the half-hour ritual might undo the vibrant glow I felt after the shower, I stopped saying the prayers. Though I decided a month later that the showers were no longer necessary, I never resumed my daily service.

Rose insisted that my collapse was directly caused by Pop's terrifying outburst. I was sure that she was wrong. I never told her or anyone else in our family about my fears of homosexuality or unmanliness, but I remained convinced that these and these alone had led to my disastrous state of mind. Moreover, I was sure they had arisen out of the blue. I had not let Willie or Dr. Madonick know about my father's episode of rage, because I saw no relationship between it and the problem for which I had seen them. The obsession with sexual identity seemed a thing of its own, unrelated to the life I had led or to any event that had ever taken place among us there in apartment A. Certainly, I thought, it stood by itself; nothing my father had done could possibly have contributed to it. Of this I was without any doubt.

IX

In America, Meyer Nudelman was a man with no past. He had left behind in Novoselitz not only his family but every reminder of it that might have been shared with his sons. Except for referring offhandedly one day to his father having been a shoemaker, I never heard a word about any of those with whom he had shared a home and a life during his first nineteen years. Once or twice, he told of swimming across the nearby river between Bessarabia and Romania with other boys, but that was all I knew of those early times. He never spoke of his parents or of the brothers and sister in those two photographs under plate glass on the dresser. The pictures must have reached him long after he left home, but how he got them is unknown to me. I have a cloudy recollection of being told, by someone whose identity is now lost to me, that he never communicated with anyone in Novoselitz after settling in New York.

Almost as remarkable is the fact that neither Harvey nor I ever asked our father any questions about his family or his upbringing. The photo of the stalwart and handsome young soldier excited my thoughts to a certain pride, and yet I never made the slightest inquiry about his story. Novoselitz seemed not to pertain to the history of what our family was.

There were reasons for the lack of interest in our paternal

heritage, and one of them was paramount: Harvey and I were Bubbeh's grandchildren, and the lore of her people was the lore we inherited. She and Aunt Rose and Momma often spoke of the events and people inhabiting their memories of Novaradugk and its surrounding towns. I was familiar with a large cast of *mishpokhe* and *landsleit,* and even with peasants, priests, and landowners on whom I had never laid eyes. They existed in my imagination, which was nourished by their tales. They had re-created their earlier life in vivid detail, and had passed it on to Harvey and me, the American generation.

The absence of so much as a thimbleful of curiosity about my father's family is difficult to explain. Bubbeh's emotional hegemony notwithstanding, my lack of interest bespeaks something of the same distancing, I suppose, that I tried to achieve at those many times when Daddy and I walked together and I was particularly determined not to be identified with him. He never seemed interested in telling me about his family, and I never seemed interested in knowing. Other than the families of Willie and his brother Sol, as well as a few cousins whom we rarely saw, there were no connections to anyone or anything Nudelman, and even those few relatives were at a distance.

It may be, of course, that my father left Novoselitz in the midst of so divisive a conflict with his family that he never wanted to talk about it to his children, fearing that any discussions of home would lead inevitably to a retelling of the perhaps bitter events that had precipitated his departure. But such possibilities are airy conjecture and the product of later years of speculation. They cannot fully explain why neither Harvey nor I tried to know more; they take form only now that I attempt to understand what I have never understood.

But not all buried associations are lost. Whatever may have caused my father to separate himself from everyone and everything whose reality preceded his arrival in America, he was destined for a grim reunion with the past, and the town of his birth.

In the year or two following the conclusion of the war, information began to become available about the fate of individual Jewish communities within the wide reach of Nazi barbarism. The Yiddish press would report the information as it trickled in, with the result that many European-born Americans were gradually learning details of the methods by which the Holocaust decimated the populations of Jews remaining in the cities and villages from which they had emigrated. For my father, the tragic news came all at once.

Meyer Nudelman was not a man who threw open the door on returning home from work each evening, energetically bursting into the house to announce his arrival to anyone present. Quite the contrary: He would enter quietly and go unobtrusively to his bedroom, as though coming in below radar. But one evening in early 1947 was like none that had ever preceded it. At about 6:00 p.m., he suddenly flung himself into the small entrance foyer of the apartment, almost falling. He was clutching a crumpled and disarrayed copy of the *Jewish Daily Forward* in his upraised hand, as if to indicate the cause of the tears streaming down his face, which was contorted with grief. As the heavy door slammed shut behind him, he slapped the newspaper against his leg in an expression of hopeless desolation, crying out the immensity of his sorrow to the heavens, to each of us and to no one, all at once. For some moments, it was impossible to know what shattering stroke of despair had torn so deeply into him that it called up such wellsprings of lamentation. He stood there virtually hysterical, unable to form comprehensible words. I had never seen him this way, and I was shaken by it. Rose and I had rushed into the hallway when we heard the commotion, but at first neither of us knew what to do. Slowly, instinctively, she found a way to help. It took a few worrisome minutes, but in an unaccustomed show of genuine concern for her brother-in-law, she finally spoke the comforting words that calmed him sufficiently for near-coherent sentences to emerge. By then, she and I had taken his elbows and led him to his armchair in the living room, and he had dropped his sob-racked body into it, as though exhausted by the burden of unbearable woe. His near shrieks had stopped and he sat there weeping quietly. He stared straight ahead, and I wondered what strangenesses he was seeing. Whatever may have been the scene playing itself out in his troubled thoughts, he shook his head slowly from side to side several times, seeming to disbelieve it, or perhaps obliterate from memory the words printed on the stark columns of an inside page of the *Forward*, which he had just picked up at a newsstand near the subway station. Only gradually did he return to a full awareness of everything around him. In flat, halting sentences, the entire horrifying narrative emerged.

Shortly after entering Novoselitz, the Germans had herded all the town's Jews into their houses in the ghettolike segregated quarter. When they were certain that no one had eluded their grasp, they slowly began to drive their armored cars and motorcycles repeatedly up and down each street, pouring fusillades of machine-gun fire into the small wooden buildings. In a short time, they had methodically riddled the flimsy structures with thousands of rounds of ammunition, returning at the conclusion of their awful work to each one from which any sounds could still be heard. When all was quiet, they burned the entire area to the ground. There were no survivors. Every Jew in Novoselitz was murdered that day.

Bubbeh stood in the doorway, unseen by her son-in-law, listening with tear-filled eyes to the recounting. When it was over, she padded wordlessly into her bedroom. Rose and I did what we could to console a widower who in his late middle age had now suddenly discovered himself to be an orphan. I sat on the stuffed armrest of my father's chair, thinking that I should embrace him but feeling unsure and awkward about it. I said nothing. A few times, I tentatively touched his back with my hand and let it linger, hoping to do something that might comfort him. Rose, who ordinarily never spoke his name, called him Meyer and found words of empathy and support. At that moment, it was as though the strain between them had never existed. When Harvey came home from his after-school job at Bloomingdale's in Manhattan a half hour later, we were still sitting there. Understanding the need but not knowing why, he set himself down on the floor in front of his father and held his clasped hands for a while.

Finally, Pop got up and made his unsteady way into the bedroom he shared with Harvey, and remained there alone. Soon after, the rest of us assembled in the kitchen to pick wordlessly at supper. I went to bed that night without going in to see how my father was.

Pop was somber and quiet for several days, but in less than a week, it was as though the story of the Novoselitz destruction had never appeared. All was as before—he never but once mentioned his family again, except to tell Harvey and me that he had arbitrarily chosen Yom Kippur as the anniversary of their slaughter, since the actual date was unknown.

A few months before my father's death eleven years later, a letter in Yiddish arrived, addressed to him from Argentina. In the envelope with it was a photograph of the sender, a man in his fifties, whose face was strikingly similar to mine. He wrote to his brother Meyer that he had left Russia in the 1930s and settled in Buenos Aires, finding work as a peddler. He had never married, and he had no children. This was my uncle Avram, the only survivor of the six members of the Nudelman family who had posed in a Novoselitz photographer's studio nearly half a century before.

My father showed me the letter and we spoke briefly about its contents, but he never wrote back to his brother. By then, his handwriting in Yiddish was so scribbly that it was difficult to decipher, but that could not have been the reason for his unresponsiveness. After all, I could have done the writing for him, or he might have asked a friend to do it. I believe it was a kind of undecidedness, or perhaps just inertia, rather than a willed choice, that prevented it. The months dragged by and he did not mention the letter again, having sequestered it in the cluttered drawer of his dresser.

About six months after Pop's death, I was in London, working for a time at an English hospital. The pace was leisurely, and one evening I decided to answer Avram's letter, which I had brought with me. In my best Yiddish script, I slowly penned the response. I told my uncle of his brother's death and about Harvey and me, the two nephews whom I hoped he would meet one day. He never answered, and I was too caught up in my own life to try again.

About six months after we learned of the destruction of my father's family, Harvey and I changed our name to Nuland. By making such a statement in the way I have, the two clauses might be thought to follow one on the other as cause and effect. But the truth is far from that. We had been contemplating our escape from Nudelman for at least a year, and the time seemed to have come. I was in my final semester of high school; we agreed that it would be best for me to start college unhampered by a burden from which we both wanted desperately to be freed.

The three of us were the only remaining Nudelmans of our extended family. The uncle with whom my father had made his first home in the teeming Lower East Side of Manhattan had a son and a daughter born in Novoselitz and then two sons born in the United States. In the early 1930s, the eldest of the four chopped *Nu* off the front of his name and became Jack Delman. This snipping form of alteration did not appeal to the elder of the New York–born sons, Sol, who invented a name that was not only meant to sound more Anglo-Saxon but might in addition say something about the new American life then opening up for him as a recently qualified accountant. It was intended to serve a similar function for his younger brother, Willie, as well, who was preparing to apply to medical school at a time when highly restrictive quotas were commonplace in the nation's universities. The name would signify the beginning of a new life in a place that the family still thought of as a new land. For a purpose brimming with such promise, nothing seemed more suitable than a rearrangement of letters—absent a few—to create what the two young men believed to be something totally original, never before encountered, unique to themselves, and symbolic of their enterprise of fully integrating themselves into America. And so, Sol Nudelman invented the name Nuland for Willie and himself.

I wish I could say that Harvey and I took their name in the cause of family solidarity, but that would hardly be true. We were motivated by other factors, each in its own way overt and pragmatic.

Both of us were fed up with what we conceived to be the ludicrous sound of both Harvey and Sherwin Nudelman. The incongruity between our first and last names had been an endless source of derision for as long as either of us could remember (although not as palpably laughable as Reid Donovan Moskowitz or Fillmore Finkelstein, the names attached to two kids in the neighborhood). In addition, becoming Nuland meant bringing an end to jibes like "Hey, Noodle Man, where's your soup?" and even less felicitous turns of phrase, of the sort that come so easily to the cuttingly quick lips of teenage boys. For me, a change to Nuland meant that I would never again have to get up on the first day of a new class each semester and announce to a pimply multitude that I was Sherwin Nudelman.

Worst of all had been that terrible first day of beginning French in eighth grade, when I actually had to come forth with the mortifying near whisper of *"Je m'appelle Sherwin Nudelman"* while standing stiff and red-faced alongside my school desk at Creston Junior High School. There—where voices changed, hormones raged, and acned faces became more blotchy, oily, and infection-prone with each passing month—the teasing was out in the open. Taunting about my name was among the grievances that exploded into a few school-yard confrontations during those "If ya say that one more time, I'll make ya sorry" years. I lost a few fistfights, broke even in a few, and never had a clear-cut victory. I was not among those boys whom no one dared antagonize.

It never did seem fair that such classmates as Eugene Borowitz, Giusto Mastroberardino, Stanley Pudnos, or even Marshall Dick could get up and say their names without blinking or self-consciousness. Worse yet, Aristides Gazettus, Kalman Ilyefalvey, and Socrates Birsky-Okuntsoff elicited fewer smirks than I did. The awkward combination of Sherwin and Nudelman—Sceptered Isle and shtetl—sounded ridiculous, I thought. The utter preposterousness of Sherwin Nudelman maintained a supremacy of ridicule—or so it seemed to me. Even when the snickers were less than apparent, I imagined them.

Without the Nudelman following it, Sherwin would at least be bearable. It would no longer stand out as an extreme example of the ill-advised mentality that made Melvins of Mendels and Sylvias of Tseitels—and Harveys of Hershels. His burden, too, needed lessening.

But susceptibility to perceived ridicule was not the only reason Harvey and I decided to make the change. The other was that era's official and unofficial bigotry. Many doors were never opened to Jews, and others were slammed shut in our faces. Companies and universities let us know that they excluded "your kind," as we were so often called, or subjected us to highly restrictive quotas. The physical ghetto of the old country had been replaced by a social ghetto, and our own sensitivities made it an emotional ghetto, as

well. I have never seen a notice reading "No Jews need apply," but
I imagined invisible signs everywhere, ones that told me the equivalent or worse. Everyday experience had deepened my certainty that
those few goyim who did not hate us were at the very least suspi-
cious of our motives for virtually anything we might undertake.

The goyim we had encountered on that unforgotten journey
to Tashlich were the coarsest of them. The finest of them would
never be involved in such hooliganism. They had their own ways,
genteel and Gentile. These were quiet disdain, snide private
remarks, and those scarcely hidden policies of exclusion and quotas. Hebrews were not wanted, and in all manner of ways, they let
us know it. In response, more than a few Jews chose various
degrees and stratagems of going underground. I would be among
them. But even when in the midst of the enthusiasm of changing
my name, I was not proud of the course I was embarking upon.

At the time Harvey and I were choosing our path, I was beginning to think about medical school. It was well known that there
was no point in a Jew of Eastern European origin applying to
two of the five medical schools in New York City—Cornell and
Columbia—and there were plenty of similar situations throughout the country. Hundreds of thousands of Gordons, Rosses,
Kayes, Davises, Stones, Lewises, Coles, Shermans, Colemans, Coo-
pers, and others had acquired their very Anglo-Saxon surnames to
help them "pass."

On the morning of October 17, 1947, two young Nudelmans
with their father in tow emerged from the D train at the 161st
Street station of the IND subway line, climbed up the stone stairs
to the street, and headed for the Bronx County Courthouse on
their way to becoming Nulands.

To achieve our objective, we had enlisted the cost-free aid of
our cousin the lawyer, Sam (or Shmuel Chaim, as he was always
called by Bubbeh, who was his aunt) Simenowitz. We were to
appear that morning before the Honorable Ernest E. L. Hammer,

justice of the Supreme Court of the State of New York. Harvey and I had talked long and hard about the events to take place on that morning.

When our father said that he, too, wanted to take the new name, we urged him not to do it.

"Vy not I shoot beink Nulant, too? If Villi 'n Sol coot beink, ent mine un sons *aykhet* [a Yiddish word meaning "also"], I vant di same fa mineself. Den ve all Nulant; ve all di same."

Harvey remonstrated with him. "Pop," he argued, "it's nuts for you suddenly to become Nuland after a lifetime of being who you are. And anyway, what kind of name is Nuland for a guy like you?" All three of us knew what was meant by "a guy like you." But no one said it. It meant a man whose entire appearance and demeanor bespoke the very stereotype of the unassimilated immigrant Jew. Whatever the sound of Nuland carried with it, it was certainly not the prematurely aged, beaten-down fifty-seven-year-old garment worker who was the son of the martyred Noach, the shoemaker of the Novoselitz Jewish quarter. Neither Harvey nor I was prepared to take him on the journey into our America.

Convincing Meyer to remain a Nudelman was, in fact, perceived as a necessity by Harvey and me. Neither of us tried to fool ourselves into thinking otherwise. For me at least, the transformation of our name was integral to the process of escape. And from what was it that I was trying to escape if not Meyer himself, and his strangeness in this America into which I was so determined to liberate myself? He was the distillation of everything clinging to me, everything of which I so desperately wanted to be rid.

Deluded by egoistic fixation on our own hopes, we were ashamed of being his sons—and he had to be left behind. He must have known it. Harvey and I knew it.

Plenty of people go through life bearing a name with far more potential for embarrassment than Sherwin Nudelman and never consider changing it. They identify it with a patrilineal descent to which they proudly assert their connection, and often specifically with a father for whom their admiration is unquestioned. That was hardly true for Harvey and me. If there is a single emotion to which our determination to be Nuland should in retrospect be ascribed, we could have identified it even then as shame. To become Sherwin Nuland was to get further away, to be more free of the entangling shame I endured for my father's otherness, which became mine long before I was perceptive enough to understand how such a thing could happen. The burden of identification with Meyer Nudelman was not easily borne, and I longed to be rid of it. Such is the vanity of youth that even responsibility and a father's awkward gestures of love are discarded in its name. If I could get away from Nudelman, I could get away from Meyer.

In the final court writ that we would be issued that day, Meyer was referred to as "the petitioner." The state of New York had declared in its wisdom that any person under the age of twenty-one was, in its legal terminology, "an infant." An "adult" was therefore required to speak for us. The adult, Meyer Nudelman, was petitioning the court to add the most symbolically powerful of the many measures by which his sons had long been separating themselves from him.

The petition presented to the court had been drawn up five weeks earlier, and was signed by Meyer Nudelman in a beautiful flowing hand that was not his. Meyer's real signature being all but illegible by that time, cousin Sam, the lawyer, had taken it upon himself to do the honors usually performed by Harvey, who commonly forged his father's name on report cards, legal papers, and the like.

All of this means that my change of name is illegal. Its official status can be rescinded at any time should the state of New York wish to do so. It might be said that I am still Nudelman. And so I am.

Neither Harvey nor I was jubilant as we left the courthouse. We had taken an enormous step. Until that moment, we had not questioned whether it was the right thing to do. But now, faced with the reality, with the awkwardness of the unfamiliar, both of us had difficulty saying our new name. We weren't even sure how to pronounce it. Were we to emphasize both syllables, as Willie and Sol did? No—New Land sounded clumsy to our ears. Should we put the weight on *Nu*? That seemed better, and we did eventually choose it. But it also felt a bit disloyal at first, having a bit of a British ring to it. We would struggle with such thoughts for months, as we grew used to becoming the young men we had not been before—as we grew used to having a different name from the one our father had.

It did not help that some of our schoolmates teased us more than ever, or that one particularly resentful gym teacher (who proudly pointed out that he had never abandoned his own name, Julius Beckenstein) would gleefully poke fun at me with taunts of "Narvell," pretending to be unable, try as he might, to remember my new name, other than that I had fancified it into sounding goyish.

Meantime, something of my father had retreated even further. The hopelessly stooped posture, the unsure hands and legs, the rolling and wobbly gait, the clothes that never quite fit, the perpetual air of fatigue and worry, the accent so thick and peculiar that those unfamiliar with it had often to ask that a sentence be repeated—I had long since grown accustomed to all of them: I had spent my life watching them become increasingly more obvious. The worsening loss of sensation and control of his bladder aggravated the retention and stasis of urine, and the frequency of overflow into the rags he wore in his underpants. When I stood close to him, I could sometimes detect the faint odor of the infected dribble. It was as though he hid a dank and foul pool just inside his pants. The stench of the drying cloths on the bedroom radiators was so oppressive that I wondered how Harvey could sleep at night. Pop refused to listen to a word of protest. On the few occasions when one of us said something about the odor, he would either become enraged or respond with his usual formula, "Ahm ah sick men," and that was supposed to excuse everything.

Were this not enough, an entirely new symptom had made its appearance a few years earlier. It occurred only rarely, but it always did so with an onset so dramatically abrupt that there was not an instant's warning. It was like a sudden shock of electricity running up Pop's lower leg. He called it "mine paynts," but Willie's name for it was more descriptive. He said they were "lightning pains," and I assumed he knew what caused them, though they seemed to have no connection with anything else about the inscrutable and nameless disease. I must have witnessed those unpredictable attacks dozens of times, but their instantaneous onset always frightened me for a moment until I realized what was happening. When they hit, each time without apparent reason, Pop would all at once pull the affected leg upward, if he was sitting, and clutch his shin with both hands. If he was standing at the moment of impact, he would frantically seek out the nearest chair or the bed and fall onto it. It was always the same. His features would distort themselves into a tight-lipped grimace as he made a desperate attempt not to cry out. Instead, the sound he made was a long, deep inhalation pulled through tensely clenched teeth, his mouth drawn tightly into an elongated slash. As the pain ebbed, he pursed his lips and exhaled in a blowing release of tension. When the episode was all but over, he raised himself from the almost fetal position into which the pain had thrown him, seeming embarrassed by what had just happened. He apologized for it, looking up at me with an abashed, almost shy expression, the hint of an attempted smile on his pallid lips. He seemed drained of life at those moments. It took awhile before he was himself again.

When the bladder infections occurred—as they were then

doing two or three times a year—they caused high fevers and sometimes required hospitalization. Willie would try to control these episodes at home, but it was risky to do so, because things could worsen without anyone realizing it. One Saturday morning when Willie was off on a trip with his family, Pop became nearly delirious from an extremely elevated temperature and fell into a profound sleep from which he could not be stirred. His skin was hot and dry, and he appeared comatose, moaning a bit from time to time but otherwise quiet and virtually motionless. I would go into his room every hour or so in the afternoon and evening just to be sure he was not worsening, and Harvey slept in a bed alongside him throughout the night. At about 10:00 a.m. the following morning, Pop awakened as though from a long sleep, soaked in the perspiration that marked the breaking of the fever. After looking around to get his bearings, his first fatigued words were to ask me the time. When I told him it was Sunday already, he stared at me in wonderment and very softly said in Yiddish, *"A gantser meshles!"* ("A whole twenty-four hours!"), expressing awed astonishment at how long he had been unconscious with the fever.

In time, calcium and other minerals began to deposit on the infected debris contaminating the urine in Pop's bladder. Sharp-edged stones formed, which sometimes passed by themselves in spasms of unendurable pain as they forced their lancinating way through the narrow duct traversing the penis. When they were too big for this to be possible, the excruciating procedure of cystoscopy was required, in which a rigid telescopic tube was pushed up the passageway into the bladder in order to retrieve the stones with grasping instruments. These procedures, usually without anesthesia, became more frequent as the years passed; the hospitalizations lengthened. Because he was on the nonpaying ward service—the charity service, in fact—all of Pop's medical care was conducted by young men in training—residents and interns. They never felt any pressure to discharge patients when the acute phase of illness had passed, and once Pop was admitted, he was likely to remain on the ward for weeks.

My father never complained. Whatever the reason—the attention he received, his gratitude at recovering from yet another infection or painful stone, or the distraction from the tedium of his life now that he was less and less able to work—he seemed content to be in the hospital. Once the acuteness of the problem had been attended to, he even seemed to treat his recovery period as a bit of a vacation. The hospital to which he went was always Montefiore, one of the institutions that were part of the loose network supported by the Federation of Jewish Philanthropies. That and the hospital's location in the north Bronx meant that the majority of its patients were men and women within a generation of the shtetl or ghetto, though some were Italian or Irish. The speech rhythms of New York could be heard in every conversation, and many of them were accented in Yiddish. Willie would visit once or twice during my father's hospitalization to be sure that all was going as it should. And I would be there every Wednesday evening, as well as Saturday and Sunday afternoons, when the regular visiting hours were scheduled.

Pop demanded that I never miss one of those visiting periods. There were many hospitalizations during my junior and senior years in high school and all through college, and on each occasion, I was rarely absent during the two-hour session. Pop and I had little to talk about, and there was equally little to interest me in that large open ward, which was lined on each side by long rows of white-enameled iron beds. The immense room smelled of the effluvia associated with various kinds of sicknesses, treatments, and the inconsistent hygiene of the ill poor. I particularly remember the foulness emitted by a legless former cabdriver named Golinsky, whose habit it was to read the *Daily News* while eating his supper, all the while perched on the bedpan he was gradually filling by a series of grunting emissions.

But Pop wanted me there. He would become offended and angry if I did not show up or even if I arrived a few minutes late. In some ways, he acted like a petty monarch exacting tribute. It was easiest to do as he insisted. Sometimes I brought a book and did a little schoolwork at his bedside, but I usually just sat there with him.

It was not my conversation that Pop needed—it was just my presence. He seemed to find it reassuring, as if the earth remained in its proper orbit only if he saw his younger boy three times a week at the allotted hours. He was strengthened by it. He loved nothing so much as letting everyone on the ward know that I was his son, even if he had introduced me two or three times before. When I was taking premedical courses in college, he made sure that no patient or visitor escaped without being told of my plans for the future. He would smile broadly when speaking of such things, and his moist brown eyes glistened with the pleasure of it. He beamed with pride and took on a proprietary air that he made no attempt to lessen.

The memories of my late teens are intertwined with my memories of the large Montefiore Hospital ward shared by urology, dermatology, and neurology patients, with all their ointments, rashes, odors, and quirks. As bored as I always was, I felt at home there, and all the patients came to know me. I was Nudelman's kid, and I was going to be a doctor. In that place, these facts were enough to confer on my father the authority and status that he lacked in every other part of his life.

I graduated from high school in January 1948 and began college a few weeks later. New York University had a program that allowed completion of freshman year by a sequence of two semesters between February and September, and my entering class emerged as sophomores in the fall, at a time when many of our high school classmates were about to begin the freshman year at other schools. For me, the Bronx campus of NYU's College of Arts and Sciences was not a commuter college—it was a pedestrian college. I walked the fifteen minutes to its wide green lawns and ivied academic buildings each morning, my books under one arm and a butter-stained bag of lunch under the other, which Bubbeh always prepared for me. I did my studying as I had done it in high school—on a card table set up in the center of the living room, which at other times was folded up and stored with its accompanying four chairs behind the opened glass door to the hallway.

I had by then realized that my interests in biology were not strong enough that I could envision a career spent in laboratories. I was Bubbeh's grandson: Life meant people, and their endlessly fascinating ways. And it also meant sickness and death. At seventeen or eighteen, the image conjured up by the thought of disease was not one of organ pathology, but that of an exhausted, fearful human being with a name and a face and a family distraught with apprehension and woe. The image also included a doctor, who could enter a small apartment and, merely by having stepped across the threshold, bring calm to a scene of confusion and dread. The doctor of my mind's eye was assured and eminently capable. He walked in an aura of certainty. When he entered a room, all anxiety would be vanquished; every danger would be manageable. His very presence would foretell the fulfillment of hope.

I had seen it. Willie especially, but Leo Hochfeld, too, brought with them into apartment A a purposefulness that overcame fear every time one or the other of them arrived in response to our need. For Dr. Hochfeld, the amulet was an imperturbability that banished pessimism and impending panic. For the more assertive Willie, it was an air of energetic competence. An idealized melding of both was the man I had begun to think I could be.

Though I had considered the decision to become a doctor as early as junior year in high school, the process began in earnest when I had to fill out the NYU application form, which required the candidate to give a general outline of a career plan. Preparation for medicine was the only one of the several listed choices that conformed with the way in which I was beginning to imagine the general contours of my future—biology with people. Once classes began, I soon discovered that I enjoyed learning science even more than I had anticipated, though I still disliked laboratories.

It never occurred to me that it might be unnatural to link science with my gradually deepening fascination with literature and the uses of language. In my naïveté, they were seamlessly united. English was the key to that great American world I yearned to enter—the world where people studied science in order to understand how things really are, the world of specialized words and abstruse concepts that could not be expressed in *Bubbehloschen*. How could I be other than magnetically drawn to such things?

And in college, there was the study of history waiting for me, too. History allowed me to learn of the currents by which that greater world of my yearnings had come to be, and what sorts of people had made it what it is. Always, it was the biographies of people of earlier centuries that I was most drawn to. In my mind, science, history, and English were all of a piece. These were lofty matters, so different from the daily concerns of Nudelmans and Lutskys. At NYU, I was learning about life in the abstract. For life in all its particulars, I had apartment A, 2314 Morris Avenue, the Bronx, New York.

And I had the 183rd Street station of the IND, among other realities. No matter how far I wandered into the glorious stratosphere of English, history, and science, I remained tethered to that place, and the strings could be shortened in an instant. Every time the pavement was at all slippery, I appeared just outside the subway turnstile promptly at 5:45 p.m. to accompany my father home. If there was so much as the slightest reason he might expect me, I was afraid not to be there. Should I come so much as a minute late, he would rail at me in a rage and mutter angrily under his breath for most of the way home. Regardless of where I was or what I was doing, it was abandoned in an instant if I thought my father wanted me. No matter how debilitated and unstable his body became, he ruled over me. All the years I knew him, his weakness remained his strength.

X

Bubbeh died during my sophomore year, from complications of a stroke she had suffered a few months earlier. It was just Rose and Meyer after that, the only remaining members of the generation that pulled at me to remain at home. Overtly, nothing was said; wordlessly, everything was said. Waiting and worrying by my father's bedside in the hospital after a difficult cystoscopy or while he was recovering from a days-long struggle with the pain and fever of bladder infections, I would wonder how long his body could continue to resist the consecutive assaults being made on it. And yet, he had no lethal disease. His heart and blood pressure were normal, there was no evidence of malignancy, and his young doctors said that he could go on like this for years and years. It was during this time that I began to wish he would die.

I never admitted it to myself. But there was no escaping that undeniable feeling of letdown each time I realized that Pop had weathered yet another storm. Try as I might to avoid facing my own thoughts, I wanted to be rid of him—to be rid of the smells, of the sensitivity to perceived insult, of the outbursts of temper, which, though now only occasional, could still unnerve me, of the constant need that I be available to him—of his ever-growing dependency. There would be no liberation so long as he lived. His life was a constant reminder that I could be called back at any moment from the furthest flights of my freedom. He was more than a reminder; he was the call.

Sitting there alongside Pop during the bad hours of his illness, I would sometimes find myself thinking of earlier times. I had never seen him as I imagined other fathers to be, and yet there were recollections of those days when he still retained a degree of vigor, and even gave something tangible and strong, no matter how small, to our lives. The least significant of past events came back clearly.

I recalled, for example, the Sunday afternoon my father decided to teach me how to shave. I was fourteen at the time, and I could tell that Pop was looking forward to being my mentor in at least this one small endeavor. He led me ceremoniously to the bathroom mirror on that auspicious afternoon and positioned us side by side. We stood there for a preliminary overview, both of us surveying the coming battlefield of my face as it stared still somewhat irresolutely back into our paired eyes. I looked regretfully at my departing childhood, and Pop, too, seemed momentarily lost in thought. Finally, he leaned forward, auspiciously turned both water taps on full, and began his supervision of this rite of passage by instructing me to soap up my face with the bar of Lux that lay ready on the side of the sink.

"You shoot puddink di sup now on you fayst" were the words that started me on the way toward manhood, this time with considerably more conclusiveness than had my Bar Mitzvah a year earlier. The purpose of this initial step, my painstaking tutor gravely informed me, was to soften the whiskers in preparation for the main event. I was flattered by the implication that they needed this preliminary maneuver. While the suds were doing their supposedly necessary job, Pop opened the medicine cabinet and drew forth his shaving mug from the chaotic jumble of its surroundings, managing with his usual maladroitness to knock a few other items clangingly down into the sink. Together, we stuffed them back onto the narrow glass shelves from which they had plunged, and then Pop's hand emerged, holding the ultimate accoutrements of manliness: his safety razor and the thick horsehair brush that completed the depilatory armamentarium. I looked at them wide-eyed, not quite certain that they were really intended for my use.

I rinsed my face clean while Pop demonstrated the proper method of stirring the brush down into the soap-filled mug with just enough pressure to maximize the amount of lather it would take up. Then, having inserted a new Gillette Thin into the razor, he showed me how I was to apply the creamy stuff to my downy skin. I did it exactly as he directed, and was rewarded by the sight of my reflected visage covered over in all the right places by an even coat of thick white foam. I was beginning to enjoy myself.

Things got even better when the actual shaving began, after I had been shown how to slide a wet index finger across the bottom of each sideburn in order to delineate its edge. I cannot now remember whether Pop insisted that against the grain or with the grain was the direction in which I must never fail to move the razor, but by that point I had become so unexpectedly impressed with his surprising expertness that I did whatever he said.

When the shaving was uneventfully completed (I was astonished at how clever my father was in guiding me effortlessly across the contours of my face) and I had washed the residual lather off my face and the razor, Pop stepped back and admired the result of his instruction. He beamed with pleasure. Into that moment was incorporated the joy of all the baseball games he had never taken me to, all the chess we had not played, and all the fishing trips that other fathers took with their sons. He had never before taught me to do anything, and he would never teach me anything again—so much of what we might have been was condensed into those few moments of my father showing me how to shave.

These were the kinds of memories that sometimes surfaced

from my mind's recesses while I sat with the much-diminished Meyer Nudelman during those long hours at Montefiore Hospital. By then, his own shaving had become erratic. Almost always, untouched patches of gray and graying whiskers remained for days on his neck and sometimes very visibly on his "fayst." He seemed unaware of them, just as he tried to be unaware of so many of the small deteriorations that were eroding his years.

I would find myself thinking about other past events as well during those hours of strained waiting. It had been a long time, for example, since he had given up his daily 6:30 a.m. pilgrimage to the G&R (for Goldberg and Rodzinsky) Bakery on 183rd Street to buy fresh bagels and rolls at two cents apiece for breakfast. A few years after Momma died, he had begun to vary this routine, but only in one way: As a special treat for Harvey and me, he would bring home each Sunday morning a delicacy he called "corrin muffles." Buttering the crumbly golden muffins was an unconquerable challenge, and not really worth the required effort. I would much rather he had not bought them, but it gave Pop such pleasure to bring us these small favors that neither Harvey nor I ever said a word to suggest that he should stop. And so I struggled through breakfast every Sunday morning, dutifully gulping unspreadable dollops of butter and handfuls of adherent corn muffin bits, my fingers and lips smeared with the oleaginous residue. Sticky clumps invariably fell, the small coagula of butter-anointed crumbs littering the sports section of the Sunday *News,* which was spread out before me on the kitchen table.

To have refused something that gave my father so much delight to provide would have been to refuse him one of the few small satisfactions his diminishing life still held.

In time, Pop could no longer make the shopping run on winter mornings when the condition of the streets prevented it. At first, the intervals between these excursions began to lengthen, as each one dragged itself out into a difficult trek. After a while, he stopped them altogether. Buying the bagels and rolls became my job. In the late afternoon, I would shop for the next morning's breakfast, going to the G&R for bagels, as well as for the ten-cent loaf of rye bread that was part of supper. In small ways like these, my father gave up the few concrete contributions he had long made to the maintenance of the household.

Even as I scrutinized his haggard, whisker-stubbled face on the pillow during those times when he was slowly coming out of one of his fever-racked sleeps, I never doubted that his dominion, weakened though it was, would persist as it always had.

I had a jolting illustration of this in the summer of 1950, when I was nineteen and between junior and senior years in college. I had gotten myself a job that was different from my usual kind of employment. Over the years, I had been or would be an elevator operator, stockboy, shipping clerk, golf-course groundskeeper, tutor, glue-factory chemist, magazine salesman, and one of those green-uniformed navvies who spear trash on the grass strips along-side highways. But thanks to the help of my friend Ronnie Chapnick, who had worked there the year before, I was to spend the off-season in 1950 as a camp counselor.

Located near Rhinebeck in upper New York State, Camp Boiberik—named for a mythical town in the canon of Sholem Aleichem, the great storyteller of the shtetl—was no ordinary summer camp for indulged kids. Like so many of the socialist-oriented institutions spawned by Jewish immigrants, it eschewed religion, preferring a secular form of faith embraced with almost equal fervor. This faith incorporated two concepts, *Traditzye* and *Yiddishkeit*—which meant the nostalgia-soaked traditions of Eastern European Jewry as transformed by the enlightened comradeship of a labor-based intelligentsia. *Traditzye* and *Yiddishkeit* constituted a jumbled hybrid of history, literature, music, and variations on the religious customs that Jews seem never able to abandon, even as they insist they are not following them. As the sun went down on

Friday evenings, for example, campers and staff—freshly showered, groomed, and dressed in immaculate white—came together in joyful assembly to sing the equivalent of secular hymns, all of them in Yiddish, all of them redounding with the emotionalism that in other settings is reserved for prayers welcoming the Sabbath.

Camp Boiberik was a natural for me. Thanks to Bubbeh, my Yiddish was fluent. I had learned to read and write my *Bub-behloschen* at a Workmen's Circle school that I attended several afternoons a week, concomitantly with Hebrew religious classes. With great anticipation, I packed my summer clothes and some necessary gear in an old trunk that Willie had dragged up from his cellar, carefully including an item that represented a secret hope: With the irrepressible optimism of a nineteen-year-old male virgin, I hid among the jumble of socks and Jockey shorts a cellophane-wrapped package of a dozen Trojans. Like an inexperienced young knight expectantly embarking on his first tournament, I sallied forth to Boiberik.

The place was a revelation. Having been entrapped in all-male schools since seventh grade, I knew very few girls, and during three years of college, I had gone on no more than a half dozen dates, all of them awkward encounters with young women I had only recently met. I was completely without social graces. At Boiberik, I found easy companionship with some three dozen counselors of my own age, half of them female. The atmosphere was open and welcoming, and I surrendered myself to a kind of exploratory hedonism that I had never expected it would be my good fortune to encounter.

To my astonishment, I found that I very quickly became a popular and sought-after young man among campers and my fellow counselors alike. A few of the most attractive girls in the camp were happy to be included in my personal circle of friends, and they even competed for my attention. I also developed some warm friendships among the male counselors. It was all too good to believe. My bunkhouse was composed of an easily managed group of good-natured thirteen-year-olds, and my duties were hardly onerous.

Of course, the girls were Jewish and the year was 1950, so there proved to be certain restrictions on just how far intimacies might go. Female virginity needing to be maintained at all costs, the order of the day—and night—had to be a voluptuary activity that was the closest thing to sex we could imagine, without actually getting there. Like some of my male friends, I would sneak up to one or another bunk on the girls' hill a few times each week at about two o'clock in the morning, take off my T-shirt and pants, and slip between the waiting counselor's sheets. We then spent a blissful hour or more of naked or near-naked kissing, fondling, and nether-region stroking, experiences that taught me more about female responsiveness than I had ever learned from the novels I used to scan frequently and furtively for "hot parts."

I never did get to use the condoms; the cellophane seal remained as intact as the hymens on the hill. Some mornings, I would awaken back in my own bunk with a scrotumful of congested veins, a condition so painful that I had difficulty walking until almost midmorning snack time. But blue balls or not, the clandestine quasi-sex was worth all the nocturnal risk and all the testicular torment. And who could know? There was always a possibility that the ultimate step might be taken on the very next of those delicious expeditions.

Because I had the best Yiddish among the younger staff, I became a favorite of the camp director—Leibush Lehrer, a fiftyish Yiddishist bachelor—and the head counselor, anomalously named Sparky Frost. I was given the lead in the midseason pageant, in which I wore medieval robes and a glued-on beard, playing the twelfth-century Hebrew sage Yehuda Halevi. My campers loved their enthusiastic counselor, and I was paid hearty compliments— and tips, too—when their parents drove up from the city to visit on

Sunday afternoons. I had come upon an entirely new and totally unanticipated world of popularity and fun, and had even discovered a rudimentary form of getting laid. I was dazzled by my good luck. If there is such a thing as "the time of your life," this was surely it.

And then Pop pulled the string. A few days after the pageant, he was admitted to Montefiore with a bout of bladder stones and infection. Though he was less sick than was usual during these recurrences, the doctors felt it best that he be hospitalized, just to be certain that his condition did not worsen. He responded quickly to antibiotics, given by what he always called an "intravenience," and was his usual self within forty-eight hours. But the Montefiore ward service being what it was, he remained in the hospital.

Early in the evening of Pop's second day in the hospital, Harvey phoned Camp Boiberik and left a message that I should call back as soon as possible. When I reached him a few hours later, he apologetically told me that "your old man" was insisting that I return to New York to visit him. Harvey knew that the demand was unreasonable, but Pop was adamant that he call. "He says he needs you" was the way he ended our conversation. I was furious, and determined that just this once I would not give in. But even as Harvey's final words were reaching my ear, I knew that I would— as always—do as my father wanted.

I asked Sparky for a twenty-four-hour extension of my weekly day off and then took the train home, feeling downcast and put-upon. By the time I got off the Jerome Avenue el at the Kingsbridge station, I had lost the buoyancy upon which I had been floating during the previous magical four weeks. Disconsolately, I trudged the two blocks to the hospital, took the elevator upstairs, and slowly walked onto the ward. I could see my father standing about seventy-five feet down the room's long central aisle. He was in animated conversation with a bed-bound patient smeared with the shiny unguent that signaled a resistant chronic skin disease. It was obvious from the first instant that there was no need for me to be there. But this was what "your old man" wanted, and this is what he must have, no matter that it forced its way into the brief interlude of my Boiberik exhilaration.

Pop gave me a big smile of greeting, his eyes shining at the sight of me. He looked me up and down as if I had just returned from years on the moon, and pumped my hand with the clammy grip that always seemed in evidence when he was in the hospital. I knew that he wanted to kiss me, but I stood back to avoid it. Turning toward his smeared ward mate, he introduced me, saying, "Dis mine son Shoifn. Heese gunk be ah dokterr." There were two other men I had to meet as well, in addition to having my presence called to the attention of the execrable Golinsky, back for one of his many hospitalizations. The introductory ceremonies having been completed, Pop and I went back to his bed, where he caught me up on the details of his current bout of illness. I told him a few things about Boiberik, and we had bits of desultory conversation during the long, dragging remainder of the two-hour visiting session. I promised to return the next day.

I arrived at the hospital at about ten in the morning, though it was not a scheduled visiting period. My two hours passed exactly as they always did when Pop had recovered from an acute problem. I was bored, and wished I had never left Boiberik. But I knew that my visit was not useless. There was no question that Harvey was right: My father did need me. He seemed strengthened by seeing me, though I begrudged him even that. And I resented his using my visit to demonstrate to the other patients that his college-boy son—a premed student, no less—was so devoted to his father and so worried about his sickness that he had traveled from upstate New York *in miten derinen* ("in the midst of everything") to be with him. From all of this, there was to be gained a large measure of *yikhes,* the Yiddish word for the stature that comes of pedigree. No wonder I seethed at being forced to take part in the performance. I was not forced by Pop alone, but also by my reluctant conviction that he should have his *yikhes*—that it was one of those things I must, however grudgingly, provide for him.

I went back to camp that afternoon, resentful not only because I had been made to take an unwilling recess from paradise but on account of feeling frustrated by not being able to tell my father just how angry all of this had made me. I remained that way for days, in a self-absorbed foul mood I did little to ameliorate or hide. I sensed that something had changed—that the spell of Boiberik had been broken. The enchantment, in which I felt myself to be the central figure, had dissipated. I blamed it on my father, and that only stoked the fires of my discontent.

In the next few days, I found myself complaining about small infractions committed by my campers, things that had never bothered me before; I was irritable with friends. I seemed unable to retrieve the Boiberik-triumphant self-image I had relished until the intrusive trip to New York. My stride had been interrupted and I could not recover it. Inexplicably and to her surprise, I became indignant when attention was gently called to my grumbling by the sweet Ruthie Isaacs, on whom my affections had become focused the previous week. Playing second base in a softball game between counselors and kitchen staff one afternoon, I humiliatingly dropped a line-drive that came right at me, and I lost Ruthie in that instant—not because of the error, but on account of my fretful reaction to it.

My campers finally staged a minor revolt against my changed notion of authority, and my closest friends stopped seeking me out. Even the nocturnal visits to the girls' hill ceased, because I did not feel welcome there. I was no longer the favorite of the camp's leadership. I had lost the happy wonder of those first four weeks.

The rest of the summer was an interval of petulance and gloom. All I wanted was for it to end, and the sad poetry I wrote in the worst hours of my dolefulness did not lessen the pain. Loudly and to the derisive amusement of a few of my erstwhile friends, I sang a few false and flat notes in the end-of-summer counselor's show (I had been given the lead part just before going to New York, on the strength of my triumph as Yehuda Halevi). Even this I blamed on my father.

But other concerns appeared before long, distracting me from the final unhappiness at Boiberik. Senior year at college began, and it was time to apply to medical school. NYU was overwhelmingly Jewish in those years, and its College of Arts and Sciences was overwhelmingly premed. All of us were painfully aware that only a small percentage of our class would be admitted to medical school, and no one took chances: The usual number of applications was thirty-five for each of us.

The card table had served me well. I was certain that my grades and a high score on the Medical College Admissions Test would get me into the first-year class of either NYU or the Long Island College of Medicine, the two New York schools that appeared not to care how many Jewish students they had. Feeling safe, there seemed no harm in trying for a few out-of-town long shots, even knowing that money considerations would stand in the way of my accepting any offer that might miraculously be made. Joe Astrove had suggested that he put me through college, but a pair of scholarships had made that unnecessary. Now I planned to ask for his help with medical school.

The first school to grant me an interview appointment was Johns Hopkins. Wearing a brand-new blue suit borrowed from my friend Stanley Cohen, I did my best to appear the composed young man I was expected to be. To my astonishment and delight, I received a letter of acceptance less than a week later. Our apartment that evening was a scene of unrestrained joy, mitigated only by my not having heard from either of the New York schools, one of which I would have to go to, Hopkins or no Hopkins. Barring an unforeseeable stroke of fortune, I would need to live at home, but at least the barrier had been penetrated—I was going to be a doctor.

Pop told the news to anyone who would stand still long enough to hear him out, but he wisely made no attempt to pronounce the unpronounceable name of the institution that had unexpectedly added so much to his store of *yikhes*. Rose, on the other hand, was not intimidated by the sounds of Christendom. I overheard her on the telephone that first evening, exultantly announcing in pidgin Yiddish to her friend Becky Schiff that *"Shepsel iz arayngegangen in* [has been admitted to] *Johnsons Thompsons medical school!"*

On the Friday evening of that week, my pal Lenny Leibowitz called to ask if I had applied to Yale. When I said that I had and then asked the reason for his question, he replied that the school gave no exams. After four years of intense study at NYU, I was thrown into a frenzy of unjustified hopefulness by that remarkable news, which carried me through until promptly 9:01 on Monday morning, when I phoned the admissions office in New Haven and asked for an interview. The registrar told me to show up at 1:00 p.m. on Wednesday. Early on the appointed day, I put on Stan Cohen's suit and took the Jerome Avenue el to the 125th Street station, where I plunked down $4.30 at the ticket window of the New York, New Haven and Hartford Railroad.

After the second of my two interviews, the dean of admissions suggested that I might like to go to the tea held every day at 4:00 p.m. He accompanied me down the long corridor of the Physiology Wing, at the end of which we entered a large ballroom, beautifully furnished and carpeted. Handsomely tailored faculty wives (the eldest of them actually had blue hair) were serving tea. Smiling graciously, they chatted with medical and nursing students and professors. All the young women looked fresh-faced and lovely, and all the young men were handsome, in a clean-cut American—goyish, actually—way.

It was a scene of wonderment, and I knew I did not belong in such a place. But that feeling was precisely the reason that made me immediately decide that I *did* belong there. This was the America I had been seeking, the America I yearned to enter; this was the America for which I was certain I had been born; this was the America for which I felt sure that I was ready to abandon 2314 Morris Avenue. Specifically because it was not my birthright, I wanted Yale to be mine. There were no Yiddish accents here and no one seemed to come from anyplace remotely like the Bronx. Certainly there were no unworldly Meyer Nudelmans. To be at this school would be to fulfill the fantasy that had begun to take form when I was a small boy on those *shpatsirs* with my mother and father.

But it seemed impossible. And the more impossible, the more I wanted it. The contradictions were many, and I kept them to myself. As long as I had no letter of acceptance either to Yale or the New York schools, I could crow about this place as much as I wanted. By no stretch of the imagination would it be possible for me to get there. And yet I was sure that I somehow would.

My Yale acceptance came ten days later. It was all too flabbergasting to contemplate, especially after NYU and the Long Island College of Medicine admitted me shortly afterward. I could now go to Joe and tell him the good news.

At home, I did not dare say anything about Yale or think about my resolve to find a way of becoming a student there. Rose and Pop were certain that I would go to NYU and continue to live at 2314 Morris Avenue. In their minds, nothing would change, except that my school hours might be longer. The family would remain intact and we would rely on one another in the muddled ways we always had. My admission to medical school meant that they stood on the threshold of a significant victory after all the years of adversity. The America of so many broken promises was finally about to keep one.

Yale was so near that I could feel it inside of me, but so far that I could not touch it. It was the money, of course, that stood in the way. But now that the future shimmered so close, the pull of home began to creep into my thinking—the paradoxical pull of the very thing from which I longed to be liberated. I was needed here. In every way both subtle and direct, Rose and Pop let me know the emotional devastation my departure would cause. Though the name Yale was rarely said, it loomed above every conversation. How could they go on without me? What would life be like for them? Again and again, one or the other of them would allude to the fine reputation of the medical school at NYU. Unsaid was, How can you consider leaving this house—and us?

Of course, these were precisely the most powerful reasons I wanted—needed—to go. Yale was my great chance. I had to find some release from the oppressive aura of stifling warmth that welled up inside me every time I let myself think of them, bereft without me. Though I knew it was love, I was being suffocated by it.

I also tried to drive thoughts of Harvey from my mind. With me gone, he would be left to deal with Pop on his own. He never said a word about my dilemma, because he understood my growing determination. He must have known that a plea from him might be enough to turn the tide toward NYU and home. But he would not make it. It was clear that he could never have done himself what I was now contemplating. No matter the loss of direction that had taken hold of him after his recovery from rheumatic fever, and no matter the grumbling resentment he made no effort to hide from his father—no matter these factors or even an emotional distance he affected from Pop's illness, he was burdened with a sense of responsibility that held him bound to 2314 Morris Avenue.

And also, Harvey must have been fearful of whether he could make the separation. Though I was the son who went dutifully with his father to the synagogue on the holidays, the son who waited for the old man at the subway station, the son who took him where he needed to go, Harvey—even though he avoided those obligations by any number of stratagems and outright refusals—was the son who could not bring himself to abandon his family. Or perhaps it was just that he was the son who could not bring himself to leave home because it took a certain daring, of which his rheumatic fever and its aftermath had robbed him.

I shut out of my mind what misgivings I could, and arranged to meet Joe for lunch in Manhattan. When I told him that NYU seemed the most appropriate of my choices, he pointed out what I knew only too well: The very name of Yale bore a unique cachet. The familiar gentle smile appeared on his face as he said, "Let me tell you something, Shep. If you're walking uptown, why not be on Madison Avenue or Fifth rather than Lexington? It makes you feel better." And with that, he offered to pay the tuition and board for the entire four years at Yale. I protested that it was too much. I could not take all that money. Perhaps he might give me just a part of it to get started, and I would work after classes until I figured out some other way to raise the rest.

He would not hear of it. "You shouldn't be distracted by needing to have a job," he said. But I was as adamant as he, and to my surprise, I really meant it. "I'll tell you what," he said, responding to my protestations. "I'll pay for everything, and when you're established in practice and have ten thousand dollars free and clear in the bank, you'll pay me back." I accepted immediately. It meant that I could go to Yale.

What it really meant was that I could go to Yale if my determination for freedom was stronger than my conscience—and stronger than the tugging. When I came home that evening and told everyone what Joe had said, there was a long silence at first. I could guess what Pop was thinking: Here is Joe Astrove, once again trying to take away my son. I could guess what Rose was thinking: I'm sure Joe wants to do the right thing, but this time he's wrong. We need this boy to stay with us.

I had to make my case gradually. With less than a month to go before it would be necessary to make a commitment to one school or the other, I kept at it as gently as I could, trying bit by bit to get everyone to understand that going to Yale was a chance to reach for the highest level I could. I appealed to their vision of the future. It would open up new opportunities; it would be better for my career. In time, pride won out, and perhaps even *yikhes* played its part. First Rose agreed, and then my father. They were heart-broken, but they knew I was right. What they did not know was that I had only told them part of my reason for choosing to leave home; what they did not know was that the other part was them.

It was shortly after—or perhaps shortly before—these events that my father proposed to my aunt. As impossible as it seemed, and seems even now, after more than half a century, he actually did ask her to marry him.

It was nine years since Momma's death, and necessity had ameliorated some of the bristling animosities of the past. Bubbeh had died two years earlier, never having said a word—at least not a word that I ever knew about—to her son-in-law, but Rose and he had gradually made some sort of peace. Their conversations were always brief and concerned with household matters or perhaps an event of worldly interest, but rarely anything more. Still, a rap-prochement had somehow been achieved, and that in itself resulted in a degree of tranquillity.

I awoke one night to the sound of voices speaking Yiddish. After a head-clearing moment, I realized that Rose and Meyer were standing in the kitchen, within easy earshot of my bed in the room across the small hallway. The time was probably about eleven o'clock. The first words I distinctly heard were Rose's. "I would never want to take my sister's place," she was saying in a voice that was remarkably gentle, though the sound of it bespoke a firmness familiar to me from long acquaintance. Her meaning was as unmistakable to me as it must have been to my father: What I am saying is definitive. I will not change my mind.

Pop tried to counter the finality he surely understood only too well. Since they were living in the same apartment, I heard him say, marriage was the right course to take. It would bring them closer and be better for Harvey and me. Calmly and evenly, Rose stood her ground. I was struck by the absence of any note of affront or brusque rejection in her voice. I would have expected her to bristle at the thought of marriage to Meyer. Instead, there was a compassion in her voice that, in my now-wide wakefulness, I realized was so understated that even this most thin-skinned of men could not possibly take offense at it. She was speaking to him as she would to a friend, with regard for the hurt he would feel if her refusal came with either a cold directness or any hint of pity. Just as I would never have predicted the suggestion of marriage, I would never have predicted the sensitivity with which she turned it down.

Why would a perfectly healthy and vigorous woman in her early sixties marry a debilitated and physically dependent man like my father? Why indeed, especially in view of their long history of animus, which had only recently been overcome? Why would she want to sleep in the same bed or even the same room with this unwholesome creature of odors and urine-soaked rags? Being nineteen and obsessed with sex, I wondered about that, too. Could Meyer do It? Even if he was somehow able to, what must it be like for the woman? No, the whole thing made no sense.

Thinking about it from my father's point of view, I wondered what could have made him ask his sister-in-law to marry him, given the serious resentment that had been the predominant feature of their relationship until only a few years ago? It did not escape me that I hadn't heard him utter the word *love* in this conversation, unless he had said it before I awoke. What I had heard sounded more like he was trying to express his longing for something better—and closer.

I stayed awake for hours, long after Rose came to her bed alongside mine and fell quickly asleep. It was the loneliness, I decided—the loneliness must have been his reason. He needed closeness with a woman who would understand, and Rose was the only woman who possibly could. In later years, other probabilities would enter my calculus. Perhaps my father hoped that the emotional intimacy of marriage would break down the last barriers of his separation; would make him less peripheral; would bring him companionship and something of the empathy he had not felt for a decade and a half.

By no outward sign would it have been possible to know that Rose and Meyer had come to a reordering of their lives together. From then on, there was an atmosphere of near equanimity in the house. A tacit understanding was reached that only Harvey and I would have detected, one that enabled a bond that might almost be called harmonious. And it was a good thing that all of this took place just at that time when everything was beginning to change forever.

XI

There is one single scene from this period whose image has never left me—Rose and Meyer alongside each other, leaning out of the two adjacent windows of her bedroom and mine, tears streaming down their faces as a car slowly pulls away from the curb in front of 2314 Morris Avenue. I am waving at them from the passenger side, on my way to medical school in New Haven. There is a brave look on my face, but it is only for them. Even in the midst of my excitement, I am apprehensive about what lies ahead; even in the midst of their sadness, they are filled with hope for my future.

The car belongs to my college classmate, Joe Durante. In the backseat is Irwin Greenberg, another of my close friends. They intend to make sure that I am not delivering myself unguarded into terra incognita, where I will be lost forever, not only to them but to myself, as well. They have insisted on escorting me to New Haven and seeing me settled there. I am amused, bemused, and grateful for the goodness they bring to their self-appointed mission—amused because they are sweet and funny in their concern; bemused because I am worried about the same thing; grateful that they are with me.

In fact, I was leaving far less behind than I had hoped. Even as Joe's car picked up speed at the end of the block—with me twisting around in my seat for one last look at 2314 Morris Avenue—I well knew that I would be on a train headed back to New York within a few days. I had shared a hidden worry only with Willie: I was depressed again.

My obsessional thoughts of five years earlier, dispersed to the four winds after a few visits to Dr. Madonick and forty or fifty cold showers, had returned. They began to creep up on me in early May of senior year in college, as I entered the period of final exams for the last time. I cannot remember any precipitating factor; I remember only that the return of the symptoms made me fearful before long that I would break down completely and not be able to go off to medical school. It was tantalizing and frightening at the same time. Everything I had hoped for seemed in danger of being lost. The more I ruminated about the possibility of its disappearing before my eyes, the more the old hobgoblins of unmanliness leaped upward to taunt me. I was unworthy, they shrieked, to take the ultimate step toward the bright future that beckoned. Of course, it was also the ultimate step that promised freedom from the bittersweet tugging of 2314 Morris Avenue, the freedom I had always been so sure I wanted. It was as though I might never accomplish this; it was as though I could not bring myself to break away.

This time, I did not wait long before acting. While my preoccupation with self-reproach was not yet so all-absorbing that the turmoil had become apparent to anyone around me, I went to Willie and told him what was happening. He wanted me to see the doctor who had been director of psychiatry in his unit on New Guinea during the war, but he was just a little hesitant to make the recommendation because the man's office was located in faraway Brooklyn. But at that point, I would have gone to New Guinea itself for help, had he still been stationed there.

My first appointment with Dr. Frank Gartenberg was on Memorial Day, 1951. The annual Grand Concourse parade of war veterans—stalwart young men and a few women from World War

II, the middle-aged campaigners of the Great War, and the grizzled old men of the Spanish-American War, whose numbers had
decreased by so many since I had begun watching the march in
first grade—was just getting under way as I shambled pessimisti-
cally down the subway steps to the 183rd Street station. Because I
had just begun a vacation job mowing grass for the Parks Department, I was free to make the long trip only once a week, on my day
off. The visits to Dr. Gartenberg continued during the whole summer, but as fall approached and I had not yet rid myself of the per-
sistent demons of unworthiness, he suggested that I come in from
New Haven every Saturday. Because my sessions with him were
keeping me afloat, I decided that the long trips and the lost day
each week were the price I would have to pay. And there was another
price. Every penny I had managed to put away during that summer
went toward train fare and the weekly bill of fifteen dollars.

And so, after each Saturday-morning physiology lecture, I
would trudge the mile from the medical school to the New Haven
railroad station. Once I had arrived at Grand Central, I took the
subway to Brooklyn. Though I disappeared this way from midmorning until late afternoon every week, no one at school was the
wiser.

In the end, it was not Dr. Gartenberg who quieted the uproar
in my mind, but medical school itself. From the first day of classes,
I was having too good a time to remain absorbed with my obsessions. A new environment, new kinds of challenges, new friends
from all over the country—these were the components of my therapy. And, of course, I had left home. I had actually accomplished it,
and no terrible thing had happened.

In addition to everything else, Yale proved to be not as intimi-
dating as I had feared. I discovered that a farm in Iowa or the campus of a state college in West Virginia were just as remote in
atmosphere from a storied Ivy League university as was the Bronx.
In fact, it made little difference where any of us came from. True,

two of my classmates did fling at me some hurtful cracks about New York (in which I heard the unspoken word—*Jew*), but each of them had already impressed me as a horse's ass, so the sting was slight. And I was not much bothered, once I had met enough students in the small Yale School of Medicine of those days, to realize from my perceptions of my surroundings and a look at the published class lists that there was a Jewish quota of 15 percent—I thought such a double-digit figure to be remarkably high, considering the temper of the times. Even recognizing that almost all of the few Jewish faculty members were living as Christians had no effect on my level of comfort. After all, thought I, this is Yale, and what would you expect? The school belongs to the goyim, and they can do what they want—I'm just happy to be here. It mattered only, Jew or no Jew, that I felt a sense of belonging far greater than I had expected. I was at ease even in the lounge at afternoon tea, where I would sometimes go in order to eat enough that some money might be saved on supper.

Though I did not trumpet my Jewishness about, I arose very early every Saturday morning to recite the Shabbos prayers, as I had done each week since my Bar Mitzvah. When I was invited by an Orthodox second-year student to eat dinner three evenings a week at the home of a nearby kosher caterer, I leaped at the opportunity, supplementing those meals with salmon, haddock, mackerel, and tuna on the other days, at a small eatery near the dorm. I thought that I believed in God. It never once occurred to me that my religious practices and my unbreakable ties to home were of a piece.

I called my family from time to time, but I was otherwise free of them—or at least as free as my conscience would let me be. But with the passing weeks, it allowed me to be more and more so. By late October, I was back to being myself at my best. I stopped the Saturday visits to Dr. Gartenberg.

The curriculum for the first year consisted of anatomy, biochemistry, and physiology, each a subject taught by basic scientists, without regard to its usefulness in the care of sick people. The relevance of our course material to clinical medicine was difficult for first-year students to judge, but it seemed far less consequential than our Ph.D. professors would have us believe. I hated biochemistry, and rarely opened the textbook or attended a lecture or lab; in anatomy class, I was confronted with a cadaver each day, whose structure was the same as the structure of the patients I would one day be treating, so I had to study enough to know what I was dissecting; physiology was the only course that held any real interest for me. It was the physiology text, accordingly, with which I spent by far the most time. And so it happened late one November evening that I discovered my father's secret—a secret that even he did not know: All of his disabilities were the result of a distinct disease with a distinct name. Until that moment, I had assumed that some anonymous and quite unique process of general deterioration had been the agent that robbed his body of its control. And I had also assumed that he just let it happen, without exerting whatever act of will was necessary to slow its depredations. I thought that the same inertia that prevented him from learning to read and write English, or stopped him from bettering himself, or explained his inability to make the effort necessary to understand the country in which he had lived for most of his life stood in the way of overcoming his physical failures or at least fighting the progression of his decline. It had never occurred to me that I would ever find out anything more about it than that. How far wrong I was became suddenly clear in a single thunderbolt of revelation on that chilly autumn evening as I was grappling with the arcana of neurophysiology, the study of the nervous system.

With increasing boredom, I was listlessly making my way through the textbook pages whose general heading was "Sensory Disturbances in Diseases of the Spinal Cord." Dully unaware that I had finished reading the paragraphs on syringomyelia, I passed without thought into the succeeding section. All at once, I realized that the text concerned a hypothetical patient exactly like my father. The description of his gait was so accurate that I could visualize Pop plodding his ungainly way up Morris Avenue. The sentences flew through my brain while I began to read as quickly as I could. And suddenly, there it was: The term *lightning pain* sprang up at me from the page. I paused after reading those two words again—*lightning pain*—and I could hear the familiar sound. It ended, as always, in the prolonged whisper that was a kind of exhaled finale to the streaking bolt of anguish, an unvocalized chant so quietly passing through pursed lips that it was not audible from the next room.

Looking up from the book, I saw my father's face as it would be when the brief episode had ebbed. He raised himself from his bent-over position and, as he always did, apologized for the disturbance, looking at me with that embarrassed little smile. His features were drained of life in the same way I had seen them so many times.

I cannot recall what I felt as I turned back to the suddenly relevant text, whose words still evoked an image of my father. It must have been confusion, and that may be precisely why I cannot remember it. But I do know that whatever it was, it transfixed my eyes on the page and drove me to devour one sentence after another without looking back at the section heading to learn the name of this hateful malady. Every word hammered itself into my mind; every paragraph added a piece to the structure that was building, phrase by phrase, into an edifice of certainty. When I finally reached the end, I knew that what I had read was accurate—this was unquestionably a description of my father's disease. Only then did I look back anxiously to see the topic heading I had not noticed before. "Tabes dorsalis," it read, but those words meant nothing to me.

So I went back to review the first sentences of the section I had unthinkingly traversed, so bored by the preceding material that I had not noticed when the text moved from a discussion of syringomyelia to that of tabes dorsalis. This time, I made sure to read carefully: "The essential lesion"—and then I was struck by the reality of what I was reading, feeling like those steers in an abbatoir must feel when they are hit between the eyes with a sledgehammer to stun them just before slaughter. I read the first sentence over and over, perhaps a half dozen times. But no amount of reading would change the words, or erase them from the page: "The essential lesion in this syphilitic disease is a degeneration of the—"

All at once, I could no longer look at the text—not even one additional time. There is a Yiddish expression for the thing that stopped me: *Es iz mir gevorn fintster in di eygn* ("my eyes were suddenly filled with darkness"). I could not see, and I could not think. It was like fainting without losing consciousness—as if I were attempting to flee the truth that appeared on the page. It was like an instant of oblivion before the reality reappeared and I knew there was no escape from it. After a moment, my eyes cleared and my mind began to function again.

Syphilis. The explanation made no sense. It was stupid, wrong, impossible. When I had gathered myself completely, I pored over the entire section of text with meticulous attention. No, there was no mistake. The signs and symptoms described there were exactly my father's, including the bladder problems—nothing had been left out. Well, not exactly—the one thing missing was any mention of the psychological destruction caused by years—decades—of a gradually worsening process of physical degeneration and the slow grinding away of self-assurance and even human dignity. The text said nothing about pride brought down by a humiliating disease. There were no words there to tell the life story of a strong man who had been robbed of his manhood, or the life story of a family battered by the damage done to its father.

I was beyond tears. The sledgehammer had stunned me to

such a degree that I was without emotion. Even the respite of a brief oblivion had not quickened the deadness in my heart. I felt betrayed, not for myself, but for my mother.

Instantly, my father was distant, estranged, unrecognizable—someone I had never known and would never understand. How is a man capable of such a monstrous thing? I wondered. At that moment, I felt he deserved every one of the chronic ravages of his vagrant lust, and there was no longer anything retained for him in my store of pity. No matter the thousand ways he had failed me in the past, what I had just read in those pages was the ultimate ripping away of my shreds of remaining faith in him. And my mother, my beloved, innocent mother—what an unforgivable crime he had inflicted on her by destroying her life. And for what? Sheer self-indulgence and immorality—mindless, swinish immorality. She had been dead ten years by then, but as the shock of disbelief passed, I mourned for her as if she had died an hour before. And with the mourning, I remembered my father's grief on that terrible afternoon when her suffering finally ended.

And then something remarkable happened. Gradually, I began to recognize my father again. I pushed the book away and tried to gather my stampeding thoughts, but even though I no longer looked at the page, I was still seeing the words and reading them repeatedly, as if they were printed on a huge poster held up on the wall before my eyes. After awhile, slowly, but only very slowly, the poster finally faded away, and I began to feel something terribly painful and yet terribly gentle—and familiar, too—under my breastbone. I welcomed it as a wandering, lost soul is welcomed back to his own home, and I let it swell and rise up until it filled me. I recognized the intensity because I had felt it many times before, though I had often not realized what it was. But at that moment, I did not need to hide from its reality. This was the soft, aching effusion of longing—all at once, the fullness of my unexpected feeling of love for my father and my father's love for me. I did know him after all. At that instant, I was him and I was me and we were united in our love for Momma. And we were united in our loss. I understood both of us. But this time, for the first time, I understood something else about him, something I had never expected to know, and it made the aching greater, and the love, too. I understood the tragedy of his life.

In moments, the huge diffuseness of emotion had made its way to my eyes and turned to soundless weeping, for both my parents and for myself—and for my brother, as well. The flow of tears released the expansive force of the sweet pain of remembering, and something inside found relief. Finally, when the tears were done, I was alone again, and I realized that the room was cold. It was the same coldness I had felt while trying to concentrate on syringomyelia. Becoming aware of it brought back the reality of my surroundings. I was shivering.

It was late—almost midnight. Midnight is still early for most medical students, but well beyond my usual bedtime, though my old habit of early sleepiness had by that time extended its limits at least an hour. I needed to talk to Willie. He would know. "Willie the doctor," as we so often called him, would know.

In the corridor outside my dorm room was a pay telephone, but I quite obviously could not use it to speak about my discovery. I wonder now why I did not go to a phone booth a few blocks away, but for some reason, I decided to wait until morning, when I might speak to Willie in his office without his being overheard by his wife or me by my dorm mates. Willie was not a soft-spoken man—in ordinary conversation, he sounded like a union boss in a hiring hall, and he actually looked the part as well, chomped cigar and all. He scoffed at the vain dignity of pretentious colleagues and tried to maintain the air of toughness he had picked up as a child on the Lower East Side, but his twinkling smile usually gave him away. The only tough thing he ever did in my presence was to tease me mercilessly about anything at all that might come to his mind while we were together. I was in no mood for teasing on this night, and I probably thought he would be more serious if he were speaking to me from his office. In spite of his having often used the term *lightning pains* when we spoke of my father's symptoms, I was sure the diagnosis of syphilis would be as surprising to him as it had been to me.

After the physiology lecture the next morning, I went back to the dorm, because I knew it would be deserted at that hour. There was no need to look up Willie's number in my little book—I had phoned him enough times over the years of growing up to have long since memorized it. I know it still today, though Willie has been dead for fifteen years, and I had not called his office for at least two decades before that. I dialed the long-distance operator and gave her the number. Willie's receptionist knew me, and I was put right through to Dr. Nuland.

"Willie, I've been reading my physiology book."

"That's great, just great. I haven't heard from you since you left for medical school, not even a postcard. And now you call just to tell me you're studying? What do you need to study for? I thought you knew everything."

I ignored the admonition, and the playful sarcasm that was just a bit beyond teasing. From Willie, I was accustomed to both. I went on.

"Well, I don't know everything *yet,* but that's not it."

"So what's '*it*'?"

He emphasized the last word, not yet done with his needling. He was speaking as loudly as he always did. Willie was not, as I had hoped, inhibited by his professional surroundings. But he knew me too well to think I would call from New Haven unless something was troubling me. Very likely, he thought I was depressed again.

"'*It*' is my father. I just figured out what's been wrong with him all these years."

"Oh? So tell me, Professor."

The words began tumbling out of me, but in a subdued voice, just in case someone had slept late and was still within earshot. I would take no chances with my family's shame.

"It's tabes dorsalis. It fits exactly. Willie—my father has syphilis."

There was a very brief pause, so short it would have gone unnoticed had I not been so familiar with Willie's way of responding with instant speed to every remark. Now he spoke more gently.

"Well, I've been wondering when you'd figure it out. Took you longer than I thought. Actually, I was the one who first made the diagnosis, when I was an intern. Until then, nobody knew what it was."

So, Willie had known of my father's syphilis for almost fifteen years and kept the secret to himself, sharing it only with the doctors who provided care on the many occasions when hospitalization became necessary.

Now it was confirmed. My unworldly father, born in a Bessarabian shtetl, had come alone to the land of opportunity at the age of nineteen, got laid somewhere, and ended up with a case of syphilis. Some ten years after the early stages of infection, the so-called tertiary, or chronic, manifestations appeared in the form of tabes dorsalis. Everything about his case was right out of a textbook. No wonder I had found it in mine.

"But how? My old man, of all people! How does someone like him get a venereal disease? It doesn't seem possible."

"Who knows? Probably got horny and went to a whorehouse one night when he was still single, or maybe he picked up the wrong woman someplace. Happens all the time, even to naïve Jewish boys. Knowing your father, it must have been the one time in his life he did a thing like that. We'll never find out."

"You mean you never told him his diagnosis?"

"What'd be the point? There's no reason he needs to know. It wouldn't help him."

"But what about treatment? How can you treat someone when he doesn't even know what he has?"

"It's easy. At first, we used fever therapy on him, and then a course of penicillin in the mid-forties. Told him it would help the lightning pains. But none of that changes a thing about tabes. It'll just keep getting worse as he gets older. As far as the rest of his symptoms go, I let him think it's some generalized process without a name. He's never questioned it."

We spoke a little while longer, and he agreed to go on keeping our secret. My father never found out. I suppose it is possible he was told by any of several hospital doctors along the way, but if he did hear something, he did not let on, either to Willie or to me. Harvey died almost forty years after that phone call, and he left this world not knowing, either.

My knowledge of Pop's syphilis took away much of whatever remained of his waning power over me. As though turning a corner onto a street where I had never been, I had all at once come upon an unforeseen vista—for the first time, I could clearly see the magnitude of his burden. There was good reason that the fact of a diagnosis should make me regard him differently, and it did. His "Ahm ah sick men" took on a literal meaning, which it had never had before. I finally knew how helpless he was against the tide that had insidiously unmoored his life and then begun to sweep it away decades earlier, and in time succeeded in overwhelming him. An entire catalog of his failings was accounted for by this new thing I had learned about him. The fact of his syphilis softened the blame I had harbored and even nurtured as a form of revenge against him. Just as I now had some perception of the tragedy of his life, I perceived as well the role of unhappiness and frustration in the years of lashing out against the everyday buffetings that constantly assailed him. Unspoken, unheard, and unheeded, Meyer Nudelman's silent beseechings to be understood had never been answered. And now at last, I could begin to know that.

But old habits die hard. Though mitigated in so many ways, my father's ability to wound me never entirely disappeared. Its hold had long been far less intense than in my earlier life, and far easier to loosen, but, nevertheless, its vestiges would not give up the entirety of their strength. On medical-school holidays and my infrequent other visits home, he would sometimes affect me like an attenuated form of the volcanic Meyer of old. But for the most part, he was far more gentle than before, or so my new perception made it seem. The combination of his fading powers and my awareness of the syphilis came to transform him in my sight. Something in me resented him as much as I ever had; something in me still wanted him dead, perhaps now more than ever; but there was also something in me that forgave the small outbursts. And this, too: There was something in me that would never completely forgive the onslaughts of all those years when it had not been possible for me to know the basis of my father's furies.

Not only did Pop appear more subdued and even gentle; he seemed able to express his affection for me in ways I had not seen before. Maybe it was my absence from the household, but whenever I went home, he let me know in every way he could that my being there brightened his days. It showed in the sentimental way he looked at me with those softly glistening eyes when he thought I was not aware of it, in the small things he tried, in his clumsy way, to do for me, and even in the way he had noticeably begun to give in to the progressive inroads of his disease. It was awhile before I realized what was happening, but the fact finally was inescapable. The fires were banked. The campaigns were over, and he was reconciled to having lost. His only victories were his sons. Harvey had not yet found himself, but I seemed to be on my way. Pop let himself fall into what I can only describe as a perpetual state of convalescence from a difficult life.

In these ways, my father gradually surrendered himself to the decline and slope of aging. He would spend long hours absorbed in the new fascination of television and be equally entertained by any of its grainy offerings, no matter how inconsequential, from wrestling (of whose authenticity he was convinced) to commercials. In good weather, he often ensconced himself in front of 2314 Morris Avenue on a folding chair that he laboriously brought downstairs from its place behind the living-room door, squinting in the bright sun and amiably greeting "naybrids ti me" as they stopped to chat. He spent increasing amounts of time sitting on a counter stool at Raphaelson's candy store on 183rd Street, a mom-and-pop enterprise that was his equivalent of a Central European coffee shop, with a cherry soda standing in as the drink of choice. Meyer had toiled at the sewing machines of some half a dozen dress manufacturers over the decades, the years of his employment in each company becoming progressively fewer as his ability to do the work lessened. If operators were let go during a slow period, he was always among the first. When his last boss—the owner of a company manufacturing inexpensive maternity garments, which he called "EZ-On Mahtoinidy Dress, ah chipperr line"—went out of business, he found himself unemployable, and he seemed relieved.

In giving in, Meyer even developed a bit of a sense of humor about his situation. Or perhaps it might better be termed a sense of irony, especially considering an exchange he and I had one day when I was trying to cajole him out of a blue mood brought on by one of his occasional ruminations about waning strength. "But, Pop," I remonstrated, "you're made of iron." He answered in Yiddish, "Oy, Shepsel. Ikh bin take gemakht fun ayzin—Ikh ken zikh nisht beygn" ("You bet I'm made of iron—I can't bend"). He was so pleased with himself for thinking of such a quick rejoinder that I would from time to time take us through it again, telling him that he was an iron man, just to give him the pleasure of repeating it.

Perhaps because he was living at home—and that in itself drove him to seek some relief from our family's difficulties—

Harvey was making a determined effort to separate himself from everything that went on in our apartment. When not working at his job with an accounting firm, he spent every free hour among a circle of friends whose spare-time activities seemed as aimless as his own. Together, they pursued an endless cycle of sybaritic pleasures, and he was rarely in the house. Rose and Meyer disapproved of his friends, they disapproved of a behavior pattern they considered dissolute, and they disapproved of the way he seemed to be wasting his life. Now that I was far away in New Haven, my goody-goody image, enhanced by the distance, became more burnished than ever. In their eyes, Harvey was the prodigal and I was the prodigy.

Pop loved to have me at home during my brief visits. He tried everything he could to please me, especially by doing small things like shining my shoes when I had not asked him to. Episodes like the "corrin muffle" ones became more frequent. Among them was the preparation of chocolate pudding.

In our home, chocolate pudding was known as My-T-Fine. I never knew it was a brand name until I chanced to look at a box of it when I was fourteen. But however called, I adored having it for the part of the meal my father inexplicably called "rezoyve." In fact, I had relished a gourmand's passion for the creamy brown texture of the stuff since the first time I'd tasted it as a small boy. The saga of Meyer and the chocolate pudding began my first year in medical school, when I called from New Haven one evening to say that I would be arriving home the following afternoon for a brief between-semesters break. When Pop asked me if I would like anything special to eat, I told him that nothing would please me more than some My-T-Fine. The result was that I came home to six cups of it, and a father immensely pleased that he had figured out how to prepare it for me on his very first try at any sort of cooking. To have left so much as a taste of it uneaten at the end of my three-day visit would have been like turning down the crumbly Sunday-morning offering of so many years. By the time I went back to school, not a bit or even a smear of chocolate pudding still stood in the bottom of a single cup. Knowing that my father craved the approval of what for him were herculean efforts, I let myself fall into the trap of telling the proud chef how much I enjoyed the fruits of his labors. I did not have the heart to do anything less. Anything less, in fact, would have been beyond ungrateful; it would have been cruel.

Even with the knowledge of what I was letting myself in for, I had no choice. From then on, there would be an abundance of chocolate pudding—cups and cups of it—waiting for me whenever I came home. If I planned to stay longer than a few days, I would open the refrigerator door and find its entire bottom shelf lined with the prepared contents of multiple boxes of My-T-Fine. Finally, having on one occasion made the mistake of wolfing the whole collection down in my first forty-eight hours at home in order to be quickly rid of it, I learned to make the cups last until the day I left, lest I ever again suffer the experience of my father cooking up a second batch. I could not ask him to stop. One night in New Haven, I dreamed that he had prepared a bathtub full of what used to be my beloved dessert. To this day, I cannot dip a spoon into chocolate pudding without seeing Meyer sitting across the table from me, his smiling face filled with the pleasure of proprietary pride as he watches me at my first meal at home, scooping up the offering he has taken such pains to make for me.

All of these decades later, I wish I could say that the new understanding of Pop's sickness and my consequent recognition of just how far he had receded into a kind of quiescence helped me find some tolerance for the publicly conspicuous elements of his disabilities. But that did not happen. He was no less an embarrassment to me than he had ever been. The steady worsening of his condition more than balanced my changed perspective about it. I felt as though in a chronic state of humiliation, relieved only by the

fact that his distance from New Haven prevented my being identified with him.

And so, I did not become less embarrassed by my father as I
grew older and thought I was growing more mature. If anything,
his steady deterioration and my increasing involvement with the
world outside of the Bronx only increased my discomfort when he
and I were with strangers. My shame—for it *was* shame—became
more severe as my circle of friends came to include young people,
and older ones, too, who had never encountered anyone like him
before. But at Yale, I was safely away from him. There, I could be
free to play the worldly and even WASPy medical student, unhampered by any associations with the reality of a father like mine. For
me, New Haven was in every way a new haven. Meyer Nudelman
could not reach me there. Or so I thought.

I was wrong.

I had found my first real girlfriend shortly after coming to Yale.
Maria Angeletti was a nineteen-year-old student nurse from a
school in Rhode Island that was affiliated with the New Haven
Hospital, where she spent a semester. She was different from any
of the complicated Jewish girls I had known at Boiberik or anywhere else. I would catch myself gazing at her in a kind of wonderment, amazed that such a person existed. Maria's shoulder-length
black hair was thick and wavy, and she had an open, happy face
that lighted up with a brilliant smile when something pleased her,
which was often. She laughed often, too, and her laugh pealed like
a newly cast church bell on a clear morning when the sky is blue
and the angels are overhead—the little angels, as in Angeletti.
Those smiles and that laugh made her dark Italian eyes sparkle
even more than they did when she was looking only at me. She
was sexy without knowing that she was sexy.

One weekend I traveled to Westerly, Rhode Island, and met
Maria's parents. Wonder of wonders, they loved each other exul-

tantly. They were the center of a large company of her sisters, brothers, uncles, aunts, and immigrant grandparents, all of whom rejoiced at being with one another, behaving in a loquacious, impassioned Calabrian way. Her family was everything that mine was not.

I called her "Doll," and that probably said more about our relationship than any analysis I might have made of it. Even then, I knew that I was playing with her goodness; her place in my life was not meant to last. And yet, looking back on those halcyon times, I believe I must, in that unthinking, self-absorbed way of immature young men, have been in love with her. But I never knew it, and so I never said it. I told myself that she was my first shikse, and that was all.

Maria and I were happy together, but our idyll lasted only six months. It was interrupted by the conclusion of her semester at the New Haven Hospital. She returned to Providence, but whenever she had a long weekend off, she would pack some extra clothes and come to New Haven for the two free days. It was during one of those weekends in late April that Meyer undertook the difficult expedition via subway, railroad, and taxicab, showing me that I was still within his reach.

It was about 11:30 on one of those glorious Sunday mornings so well known to young lovers in the midst of the first affair of their lives. Maria and I had had two long, blissful nights together, and we had lingered in bed as late as we could that morning, until the growling demands of hunger forced us to get up for a late breakfast. We left the room in disarray, the bed unmade, and stockings, shoes, and underwear strewn all over the floor, a consequence of our hasty undressing the night before. The odor of lovemaking, still new and wonderful to us, permeated the room and clung to our bodies.

I lived on the first floor of the dorm, a scant thirty feet from the entranceway. As we opened the outer door facing on the street, we were greeted with the improbable sight of my father's hunched back. I could not believe what I was seeing. Not knowing which was my room, he had been sitting patiently on the front steps for an hour, enjoying the sun, as he so often did on the folding chair at 2314 Morris Avenue. Hearing the door open, he turned his body around as much as he could and grinned up at us, obviously pleased to have caught me unawares. "Pop!" was all I managed to gasp.

I helped him to his feet, and all three of us stood there for long seconds—Meyer looking from one to the other of us like an approving old-world rabbi, I still too dumbfounded to say a word, and Maria smiling warmly, as she always did when about to be introduced to someone she wanted to meet.

But I made no introduction. Instead, I sputtered something about the unexpectedness of finding Pop there. I was as flabbergasted by his presence as I was by the sequence of obstacles he had obviously overcome in order to reach the spot on which we were standing. For a moment, I was too shocked to be embarrassed, either by his presence before Maria or her presence before him.

Maria sized up the situation almost immediately. After taking Pop's hand in greeting and gently holding it for a few lingering seconds, she said a few words about having to be somewhere else, excused herself, and walked off briskly, as though rushing to a noon Mass that was about to begin. After watching her disappear down the street, Pop said that he had been looking forward to seeing my room. There was no way out of it, so I took him inside, breathing a sigh of relief that no other students were in the hallway. He looked around superficially, probably reassured when he saw that I was not living in a sty. He seemed not to notice that the place had the appearance and the musky odor of exactly what it was: the disordered scene of the morning after a night of making love. And then he said, "Dot's a byuriful goirl—you mebbe gunk merry mit huh?"

I explained that Maria, as "byuriful" as she was, was not Jewish, and therefore to "merry mit huh" was out of the question. Pop was very obviously disappointed. "Sotch a goot-lookin kit," he offered a bit regretfully, and his voice trailed off into a brief silence. I was relieved when nothing further was said about her.

I looked up and down the street, feeling easier once I saw no other students or anyone else to whom I might have to introduce the bent, tired-looking shtetl Jew with whom I was standing. Now my problem became to take him off to a place where I could avoid seeing any of my friends. Some months earlier, I had told him about an eatery a few blocks away on Oak Street, Greenberg's Ideal Kosher Restaurant. Slowly and with great effort, we made our way there, Pop's fingers pinching my skin as they always did. I dragged out the lunch as long as I could, and then asked Greenberg to phone for one of New Haven's few taxicabs. Pop and I had spent two hours at the restaurant and been seen by no one except the usual denizens of the place, a group of thick-accented men very like my father, absent his disabilities. Our conversation had little to do with school, most of it being concerned with home, complaints and worries about Harvey ("ah regelerr goot time Cholly" was how Pop despairingly described his elder son), and an assortment of other trivia that I thought of to make as much time pass as possible. My aim was to eat up the hours so that we would not have to visit the school or go back to the dorm. Pop and I might have been talking in a cafeteria on Fordham Road, so hermetically sealed were we from the ivied reach of my new life. Yale did not penetrate the Bronx atmosphere that surrounded us in this sanctuary. It was Greenberg's, it was kosher, and, for my purposes, it was ideal.

The strain of trying not to be seen with my own father disappeared when I had put him back on the train to New York. He had

had a good time, he said, and was glad he had come and gotten the chance to see how I was living. I made him promise never to take me by surprise again, and he agreed. I felt like I had narrowly averted a disaster.

Concerned about Maria, I walked back to the dorm as fast as I could. She was waiting in my room, having circumnavigated the block a few times until she was sure that Pop and I were gone. The bed was made and all the debris of the night before was in its proper place. Her face opened into its joyful smile as soon as I came through the doorway, and she leaped up to throw her arms around my neck. I mumbled some words of abashed apology, but she shushed me with a finger pressed against my lips. "He's so cute," she said, "and anyway, he's your father. I'm really happy he came." She could not understand why I was so ashamed of him.

XII

___

As pleased with the accomplishment as my father was, it took days for his exhaustion to lift completely. When I phoned on Sunday evening to be sure he had arrived home safely, he pooh-poohed my concerns, but a week later he was ready to talk about his adventures to and from New Haven. He described the entire journey in a detailed travelogue, mentioning all the hazardous moments. In retrospect, he was astonished at what he had done. It was not, he said in a voice both amazed and amused at the difficulties he had overcome, something he was likely to try again. Pop kept his word. During the three remaining years of medical school, he never once undertook another junket to New Haven.

Who knows if the promise would have been kept had the journey been easier? Seeing how I lived was not my father's real purpose in making his way to my dormitory; he had come because he missed being with his son. I could tell this from the cursory glance he cast at my room that day, and the tenderness in the way he looked—*gazed* might be a better word—at me; I could tell it from the things he chose to talk about, which had everything to do with home and little to do with Yale; and I could tell it from our physical connection as we walked, which, though necessitated in part by his instability, brought a sense of his warmth to me as it rarely had in the past. His clinging hand, his arm, his body rocking even closer than usual against mine as we laboriously negotiated the New Haven streets dissolved for a while the distance I had been trying to create and restored a feeling of continuity, reminding me of all the years we had spent together. For those few hours, we were as we had always been and yet never had been, without the rancor and without the pain. Even my anxiety at being seen with him did not lessen the communion between us.

But those momentary feelings quickly passed. As soon as Pop's train left the station, I was back to my New Haven self. As long as the geographic divide was maintained, I basked in the aura of autonomy that had steadily increased during the months following our leave-taking the previous September. The distance from New York brought the remove I had so long sought, but it never brought a gulf of total separation. Nor should I have expected it would. I was too much a child of my family, too much drenched in the bittersweet world of 2314 Morris Avenue, too much the product of the memory of the shtetl, and too much imbued with and at the same time supported by the old emotional burden and its underpinnings to allow the completeness of separation I had always pursued. Both besmeared and adorned by home, I was suffused with a wistful yearning for the place and the people I could not leave, a yearning that refused to yield to my relentless drive to be free of them. Something of me would always be homesick.

Had I ever doubted that a fully realized separation was impossible, my father's recurrent bouts of bladder stones and infection would have convinced me otherwise. During the four years of medical school, the periods between hospitalizations grew shorter and the severity of the episodes became greater. While I could no longer be at his bedside for every visiting session, I would manage to get there a few times during each three- or four-week hospital stay. It was around this time that Pop's hair began defying nature, or at least nature as it is described in textbooks.

I have more than once read that the phenomenon of hair turning white or gray overnight is the stuff of old wives' tales. There is no physiological way, say my unimpeachable sources, that such a thing can happen. Except for a tiny bit at the follicle, hair is not a living substance. Its color is imparted by pigment incorporated into the cells before they die. No change is possible until growth at the base of the shaft pushes newly formed hair outward. Dermatologists scoff when they hear reports that illness or extreme stress has accomplished what their scientific knowledge assures them cannot happen.

And yet, I twice saw my father's hair change color in a period of less than twelve hours. Meyer's hair had become slightly gray as he reached his early fifties, but most of it remained dark in color, though somewhat faded from its richness of earlier times. Even in his middle sixties, he might have been described as having grayish but not gray hair.

Each of Pop's two flights in the face of human physiology took place when he was admitted to the hospital with a raging fever and dehydration so severe that confusion had set in. Antibiotics and fluids had been poured into him in high volume by "intravenience," so that he was much improved by the following day, when I arrived on the ward to visit him. But both times, his hair had turned completely white. It would take weeks for the color to return. But after each episode, it came back somewhat grayer than before. Even in this, the defying of nature, Meyer Nudelman was sui generis.

Of course, the sense of being different that pervaded my perception of our family did not come from Pop alone. The difficulties with English, the lack of assimilation, the looming aura of yet another tragedy to come, the perpetual envelopment in pessimism—all of these had been shared by Lutsky and Nudelman adults since my earliest awareness of them. Though my father was the exemplar, I viewed with shame everyone who had brought me up.

Considering all of this and especially my feelings about Pop, I did not relish the thought of medical-school graduation day. As the time approached, I became increasingly apprehensive that I would be exposed as far more the son of the shtetl than my Yale classmates might have guessed. My recollections of Pop's surprise visit did not reassure me.

But when the day finally arrived, its events proved a lot easier to contend with than I had feared. Harvey and Arline were there, and the distracting presence of Arline's precocious two-year-old daughter further alleviated my concerns. And there was something else: The parents of a few of my classmates were immigrants who spoke with Eastern or southern European accents—one couple even in the unmistakable tones of Yiddish-tinged English—which marked them as working-class people. Except for the blessedly few words spoken by Rose or my father to several of the graduates or their relatives, they were almost lost among the crowd of guests, who, in any event, had more joyous things on their minds at that celebratory time. Harvey or I stayed close to our old man, so that even his ungainly movements were probably not noticed by many people.

It was a proud moment for Rose and Meyer, and they glowed not only figuratively but literally, too. Every time I looked toward one of them, I saw a face wreathed in a wide smile, and eyes that shone. Pop's glistened a deep brown, expressing the sheer pleasure of the moment; Rose's sparkled bluer than the brilliant sky on that cloudless day. For the first time among strangers in a public place, I was unaware of feeling embarrassed by my family. In fact, one of my current girlfriends, graduating from the Yale Nursing School without her far-off parents, spent an hour with us, and I barely remembered to consider what she must be thinking of my father.

Perhaps my comfort was part of the euphoria of the day. A kind of magic surrounded everything about it. I was a doctor at last, and would begin training as a surgeon in three short weeks, here at the same fearsome Yale that had caused me such trepidation only four years earlier. In that brief time, I had made it my own.

But for me, graduation was only a brief interlude in my long pilgrimage toward a different kind of life. I went home to the Bronx for a brief pre-internship vacation after graduation. There in apartment A, I spent my last extended period with my family, surrounded by memories of the past and the activities of the present. Harvey, at twenty-four, was doing well in the accountancy firm, where he was at last finding a focus for his restless energies. Rose, at sixty-eight, went as vigorously as ever off to work in the Garment District every day. My father, at sixty-five, had long since withdrawn into the long and gradual gradient of aging. I ate a great deal of My-T-Fine.

Every once in a while during those weeks, Pop and I would have a small squabble about something or other, but by then he was acting more like the party being hurt than the one doing the hurting. In moments of friction, I several times blurted out a sentence of discontent or accusation that wounded him, so far had the shoe moved toward the other foot. He might then sulk for a while or perhaps mutter a few words about life having become so difficult that it was hardly worth enduring any further. Sometimes he repeated the slogan he had long been invoking against Harvey or me, his anger now in large part replaced by appeals for sympathy or attempts to make us feel guilty about our behavior toward him. "Ahm gunk c'mi soozih," he would grumble, but it was not possible to take his suicidal threats any more seriously than we had in the past.

I had surprised myself by becoming fascinated with surgery in junior year, during the twelve weeks of my student rotation in that specialty. Of all the branches of medicine, this was the one I would least have predicted might be my career choice. But I came under the influence of a charismatic senior resident who approached the surgeon's craft as an aesthetic undertaking. Caught in his spell, I saw that an operation could be both an art form and an intellectual exercise. In surgery, the thinking mind and the aesthetic sense come together to bring about a kind of technological beauty in the service of healing. The way an operation is performed, he showed me, is the expression of a surgeon's personality and his commitment to the art. After no more than two weeks under his encouraging tutelage, I was determined to become a surgeon.

I was well aware in starting the Yale program that I faced discouraging odds against completing it. The surgery department accepted thirteen interns each year, only two of whom would rise to the top of what was called "the pyramid system," to become chief resident in the fifth and sixth years, a job that opened wide the portals for any career path a young surgeon might choose. By then, the other competing candidates would have been encouraged to seek positions in a lesser surgical program or to transfer to some other specialty. The means of dropping a young doctor from the Yale pyramid was to let him know that his contract would not be renewed at the conclusion of the year, a discovery he made when he could not find his name on the list of reappointments posted on a bulletin board outside the chairman's office early each December. It was a cruel system, but each man embarking on it knew what he was taking on.

And we also knew that ability was not the only criterion. It was well understood that the Yale chief surgical resident was traditionally cast in a particular image, so specific as to be a virtual stereotype: Supremely confident, he was a born leader and the sort of fellow who reflected well on the tradition of many generations of such surgical Frank Merriwells. As inadequately as I yet matched the mold, he was the man into whom I was trying to shape myself.

There was another criterion as well, one openly discussed only among the few Jews who had made their way to the ascending levels of the pyramid. It was necessary to be a goy, and preferably a

Protestant. The last—and only—Jewish chief resident at Yale had been appointed in 1939, and it was no secret that he had abandoned his religion and was raising his children as Christians. But there was a glimmer of hope. One of the two chiefs taking over as I started my training was a very obviously Jewish-looking veteran of World War II named Ira Goldenberg. I would work as hard as I knew how, and hope that the landscape was beginning to change.

But I needed more than hope. I did everything I could to act the role that nature and nurture had not assigned me. Though my fellow residents knew I was Jewish, my appearance and a certain evolving surgical confidence gave me something of the mien of the wholesome American boy that I hoped my goyishe teachers would take me for. I was, after all, Nuland and not Nudelman. If they assumed me to be one of them, I had no intention of disabusing them of such a notion.

But still—though I had stopped eating kosher food during senior year of medical school—I awoke even earlier than usual on Saturday mornings, put on my prayer shawl, and read the Shabbos service in the safety of my room. It could not be abandoned, any more than 2314 Morris Avenue would allow itself to be completely abandoned. I was one thing to my friends and quite another to the professors who were to make decisions that would determine the course of my career. It was their game I had entered, and I would play it by their rules. Despite the anomalous presence of Goldenberg, I saw no other way to win.

From the very first day of internship, I loved the life of a surgeon. I loved being with patients, I loved the operating room, and I loved the sense of camaraderie that pervaded the resident staff. Though I often began the morning's activities before 5:00 a.m. during that year and the three succeeding it; though I rarely came off the wards before late evening of the following day, only to begin again some eight hours later; and though I usually got no more—and sometimes a good deal less—than four hours of sleep during that long interval of continuous duty, I thrived on it. The period of training was a time of my life when I was palpably a better doctor at the end of each day than I had been at its start. It was a constant happy turmoil of learning and doing. I could feel myself changing from week to week.

The intensity of the work kept me from more than the briefest contacts with home. I would make an occasional phone call and every few months go to the Bronx for a visit lasting about twenty-four hours on a weekend, but I was otherwise completely absorbed in the hectic pace of my training—and, although I would have denied it, in myself. That series of four single-minded years was a frenzied, passionate time. I lived it on a mountaintop of astonishment that surgical skills came so naturally to me.

But there was still my father to draw me back, and the exacerbations of his disease. By the middle of my internship, it was becoming increasingly difficult for the doctors at Montefiore to treat the infections. His bladder had lost almost all of its remaining ability to contract. It would retain its turbid urine in a fetid, debris-filled pond of stinking toxin, stones, and microscopic shreds of shed tissue. The far bedroom smelled worse than ever. Pop was stuffing more old cloths than before into his underpants, even as the worsening control of his hands made it ever more a challenge to wash the rags. The stench had become unbearable.

Not only that—some of the stones had proved impossible to grasp or crush through the cystoscope. Pop had required major surgery on three separate occasions, during which his bladder was cut open and the stones removed. Though the wound healed without complication each time, there was a limit to the number of incisions that could be safely made through the same area.

But the real hazard lay in the possibility that one of the recurring infections might prove uncontrollable. Pop's life was endangered every time the floods of bacteria forced their way from the backed-up urine into his bloodstream, to be carried to every distant part of his body. The only way to avoid such episodes of blood poisoning would be to provide some means of draining the contaminated urine in order to prevent its accumulation and relieve the pressure. This would require an operation to insert a wide-bore rubber tube, which would pass from inside the bladder out through an opening made in the abdominal wall just above the pubic bone, then enter a plastic bag strapped to Pop's left thigh. The rerouting would have to be permanent.

It seemed an extreme measure, but there was no choice. The doctors suggested it first to Willie and then to me, and we gradually convinced Pop that he had to accept it. He could never quite comprehend the rationale, but he finally assented, saying with a chuckle that it was enough for him that Dr. Nuland and Dr. Nuland agreed that he should have the operation.

But he was Meyer Nudelman, which meant that inevitably there would be problems. On the morning of the planned surgery, I received an urgent phone call from the urology resident at Montefiore, who told me that a "one-in-a-million mishap" had occurred. As anesthesia was being administered, Pop's larynx had gone into an intense spasm, which proved impossible to stop or relieve. The laryngospasm caused such constriction that neither oxygen nor a breathing tube could be forced past the vocal cords. Only a very quick and skillful tracheotomy had saved my father's life. He was back in the recovery room, the resident reassured me, breathing easily via a curved metal tube, which had been inserted through the hole cut into his windpipe below the vocal cords. When I asked the cause of the spasm, the resident replied that it was thought to be a highly idiosyncratic reaction to the pentothal—"one in a million," he repeated. Here, too, Meyer Nudelman was sui generis.

I was off duty the following weekend. When I arrived at Montefiore, Pop was sitting up in bed and unable to speak without placing a fingertip on the opening of the tracheotomy tube. One of the characteristics of tabes dorsalis being an inability to locate one's hands and fingers without looking directly at them, this was proving to be particularly difficult for him to accomplish. But he was taking it in good humor, especially when he found himself wandering onto his nose instead of the intended target, or sometimes missing his face and neck entirely and going past an ear. It was easier for me to take his outstretched forefinger and put it in the right place when he wanted to say a few words.

In spite of having had the details of his reaction to the anesthetic explained to him, Pop had no real idea of what had happened in the operating room. Without questioning it, he accepted Willie's explanation that it had been unforeseeable and therefore unpreventable. His uncomplaining response was in keeping with his responses to all of the indignities to which his many hospitalizations and surgeries had exposed him. He was always remarkably good-natured about everything that happened, and he tried in every way possible to be as helpful to the doctors and other staff as he could. When a new intern came to draw blood or insert an intravenous line, for example, Pop gave him helpful pointers on how to do it. Student nurses and aides were treated the same way. Personnel at every level, from orderlies to senior consulting physicians, adored Pop, and some would compliment me on having a father with such a sunny, imperturbable disposition. To all of them, Mr. Nudelman was the ideal patient—patient, in fact, with everyone and everything.

I would marvel at it, sometimes disbelieving the evidence before my eyes. Imagine: My volcanic father of old, transformed into the very model of benignity, goodwill, and never-failing thoughtfulness. Even his changed ways at home did not approach matching in magnitude or quality the extent of his goodness in this place.

Pop stayed in the hospital until his tracheotomy tube could safely be removed about ten days later. When the wound had healed, he was taken back to the operating room and the supra-

pubic cystostomy, as the procedure is called, was successfully performed, without any recurrence of laryngospasm. He recovered
uneventfully and was home three weeks later. From then on, the
urine drained easily into the bag on his leg. Though he never had
an easy time emptying the collected urine into the toilet bowl, he
somehow managed it, despite the frequent mess he made of it.
The bedroom smell lessened considerably, but the price paid for it
had been high. Still, following the surgery, there would be only one
more hospitalization—for a relatively minor bout with bladder
stones. That in itself made the whole undertaking worthwhile.

On one of my infrequent visits home a few months after Pop's
operation, I noticed that Rose was constantly scratching her arms
and reaching around to her back. She told me that her skin had
been itching for a few weeks and it was becoming worse, now having spread to other parts of her body. The intensity had grown so
severe that there were marks on her forearms and behind her
shoulders. At the same time, she had noted increasing fatigue, to
the point where she was exhausted at the end of a day's work and
barely able to prepare supper. I puzzled over her symptoms and
came up with nothing until a few weeks later, when she called to
tell me that she had discovered a lump in her right armpit. I felt stupid and neglectful. Had I given it a little thought, I would have
discovered the cause of Rose's difficulties. She had a malignant
disease—lymphoma, a cancer of the lymph system.

A biopsy at Montefiore confirmed it. The year was 1957, and
the prognosis for the average patient with lymphoma was six
months from diagnosis to death. But a new drug, Chlorambucil,
had recently been introduced, and it gave us reason for hope. A
course of it did, in fact, result in complete relief of the itching and
tiredness, as well as in a regression in size of the many cancerous
lymph nodes that by then had been found in various locations in
Rose's body.

The remission was dramatic. I watched with relieved satisfaction one evening as Rose, sitting in her usual place, the stuffed armchair in the corner of the living room, cheerfully quoted the spontaneous exclamation made the day before by the usually reticent hematologist treating her. "Amazing!" she declared, imitating his pleased tone of surprise and the big smile that had accompanied it as he completed his examination a week after the final dose of Chlorambucil. "Amazing!" she repeated, because the sound of it made her glad. We were convinced that the lymphoma would not be heard from for a long time.

But we were wrong. The fatigue returned within a month and recurrent lymph-node enlargement soon followed. A second course of the new chemotherapy had no effect.

Rose never spoke of the certainty of her coming death. Consistent with the determined and stoic woman she had always been, her wish was to protect Arline, Harvey, and me from its reality. And our wish was to hide what we knew. The interplay of deceptions was ill-advised from the beginning. Aunt Rose, this extraordinary woman on whom the burden of all our lives had been placed, died when the textbooks predicted she would—exactly six months after her diagnosis had been made—without hearing the words that would have told her how much her life had meant to us. She had lived far more for others than for herself, and she died only after having survived long enough to know that we were on our way toward better things than we had been born to.

Had anyone predicted a decade earlier the profound effect that Rose's death would have on my father, I would not have believed it. Though apart in so many ways, they had grown together in so many others. A mutual dependence marked by undisguised contempt had become a mutual dependence characterized by their acceptance of each other. For my father, it was far more than acceptance. He had come to rely on Rose's stability, and he was grateful for the many ways in which she had stopped judging him and even become a supporting influence in his day-to-day life, with its concomitant difficulties. As she was a rock of strength to Harvey and me in that household, she was a rock of strength to him, and a force in holding his life together. Both of them loved us, and that fact had become a magnet drawing them closer to each other, after all the years when even that love was unable to overcome seething animosity. They had finally found their own kind of peace. And now my father was left without her.

Pop wandered about as though lost. And so did Harvey. Arline was married by then and already had three children. Her home in Westchester had become the gathering place for our family, and I increased the frequency of my visits for a while, so that we could all be together more often. In the months following Rose's death, I would see my father and my brother there every few weeks—both were distracted, each alone in his thoughts, and rudderless without Rose. Harvey had his work and his now-ascending career as an accounting executive, but Meyer had nothing. He could be roused from his sadness only by Arline's children. All the tender affection his own sons had not been given, he lavished on them. He was like a doting grandfather. Through these three, he found a new richness in his life that I marveled at. Something suppressed had been freed.

About a year after Rose's death, Pop began having pain and running a low-grade fever, caused by the first recurrence of bladder stones since his suprapubic cystostomy. He was admitted to Montefiore in order for the stones to be crushed, a procedure now much simplified by the opening that had been created in his abdominal wall. It was no longer necessary to pass a cystoscope through his penis. The minor operation was accomplished without difficulty, but Pop was nevertheless scheduled to remain at Montefiore for his usual three-week stay.

This period of hospitalization included the first two weeks of December 1958, the time in the fourth year of training at Yale when the names of the next two chief residents were to be announced.

Our group of thirteen had been winnowed down to six as we rose up the progressively narrowed pyramid. The final choice was to be made at a meeting of the senior surgical faculty, scheduled for the early afternoon of Monday, December 8, my twenty-eighth birthday. The decision would be the culmination of everything I had been working toward since leaving home more than seven years earlier.

Pop had long known that the crucial pronouncement would be made sometime in December, but there were other things to talk about during our phone conversations, and mention of the meeting never came up. And so, when the department chairman called me into his office late on the afternoon of my birthday to tell me that I was one of the chosen two, my father had no way of knowing that the long, anxious wait was over.

I called Harvey and then Arline that evening with the good news. I was overjoyed, and bursting to tell my father, but not over the phone. I wanted to see his face; I wanted to look into those expressive eyes in which, over the years, I had seen so much anger, so much sorrow, and finally so much tenderness. I wanted to see the happiness enter them, the joy that would come from knowing his son had been chosen to be chief surgical resident at Yale, a place in America he had never heard of before I left his home to study there.

My next night off was on Wednesday. Elated at the thought of Pop's reaction when I gave him the news, I started up the reluctant engine of the secondhand Plymouth I had bought three years earlier with part of the proceeds of a research fellowship and headed down the Merritt Parkway to Montefiore, where my father was recovering smoothly from the small procedure of the previous week. It was an exciting ride for me, enthused as I was with the anticipation of that moment when Meyer Nudelman of Novoselitz and 2314 Morris Avenue—Meyer Nudelman, lost in America and lost in his own life—would hear that his son Shepsel had won the ultimate prize, fulfilling the dream he had so cherished.

I parked the car at the curb alongside the hospital and bounded up the front steps two at a time. Racing across the lobby, passing slowly moving groups of visitors and the imposing bust of Sir Moses Montefiore, I reached the familiar elevator just as its shiny metal doors were about to close. On squeezing into the crowded car, I found myself standing next to Seymour Furman, a surgery resident doing his rotation in the urology service. Being two young men traveling along similar career paths, we had briefly chatted once or twice in the past. As we got off at the third floor, Furman told me that my father's recovery was proceeding smoothly and discharge might be possible as early as the following Monday.

I found Pop lying on his bed in a four-patient room across the corridor from the elevator, a bit down the hall from the large open ward. He had no forewarning that I would be there. When he looked up and saw me standing in the doorway, his face broke into a wide grin of happy surprise. Before I could say anything more than "Hi, Pop," he had introduced his surgeon son—"fin Yailss collitsh"—to Plotkin, the middle-aged patient occupying the bed on his left. The purpose of my visit must not have occurred to him, even as I drew the curtain between the two men in order to achieve a modicum of privacy.

I sat down on the side of the bed, trying to contain my excitement so as not to give anything away. When my father had propped himself up on two pillows and we sat facing each other, I said as simply as I could, "Pop, I made it. I'm going to be chief resident." He looked blankly at me for an instant, as though not comprehending the import of what was being said. Then his expression slowly changed as all his lifelong hopes began to shine forth from his eyes and into mine. I had done this great thing for all the reasons that make young men strive for success, but I had done it for him. This is what those luminous eyes were telling me. What I saw in his face was something beyond pride. It was vindication; it was fulfillment; it was the love of a father for his son—a father who was just beginning to learn how to express his depth of feeling.

I threw my arms around Pop's shoulders and made no attempt to disguise the tears. After long and emotional seconds of holding him to me and being held to him, we slowly let go of each other. At that moment, I saw that his eyes—those wonderful soulful eyes that said so much—were now beyond shining. They were lustrous. I saw long years of the past in them, and I saw the present moment of realization, in which the strands of our lives had come together in a kind of awe. I thought I could see the future. I looked into the face of my father, and saw everything there.

Pop needed no words. My triumph was his reward for all the bitterness he had suffered over the years, for the hours of despair, and for enduring in the face of sickness, pessimism, and even death. I had justified every confidence he had ever nurtured that things would someday and somehow be better. This news of mine was testimony that he had not failed in America. It was his affirmation as a man.

My father's eyes told me all of this, and then they filled up and overflowed in one of those thunderclaps of uncontrollable laughter that brought tears into them. And I laughed, too. We both babbled torrents of words for a few minutes and then sat quietly, talking about our happiness. He told me that he had always known I would be one of the chosen two. "Ahm ah shoor tink," he said, "vot you vit be di chiff."

I stayed there, sitting on the side of the bed, for about fifteen minutes. I had to get up very early next morning, and a long ride to New Haven awaited me. We embraced one more time, I kissing his grizzled, unshaven cheek and he kissing mine. Before stepping away, I pulled back the curtain between the beds, because I knew exactly what my father wanted to tell Plotkin when I was gone. For once, I did not mind.

Pop admonished me to drive carefully, and I said that I would. I should have told my father I loved him; I should have said it at that moment, just before turning to leave. But I had never done it, and I did not do it then. Neither of us had ever done it, and we did not do it then.

Standing for a moment at the foot of the bed, I raised my hand in a final wave of good-bye, and Pop's eyes were gleaming again. I looked long and hard at his face, which was saying so much to me, then turned around and walked toward the elevator. I knew that those lustrous eyes followed me until I was out of sight.

Around five o'clock on Friday, shortly after Shabbos candles had been lighted in Jewish homes all over the Bronx and New Haven, I heard the page operator blast out my name several times in rapid succession, which always meant that an outside call was waiting. I quickly went to answer it at the nurses' station and was told that a doctor from New York was on the line.

"Dr. Nuland," said a familiar voice. "This is Si Furman, calling from Montefiore."

I must have known what he would say next.

"It's about your father. I'm sorry to have to give you this news."

I could hear his distress. He had something terrible to tell me, but all he could do was blurt it out: "He's dead."

Just as simple as that—"He's dead." My father's life was over. Meyer Nudelman's life was over. And yet, I was somehow not surprised. And on the other hand, I was.

"But how? What do you mean? It can't be."

"We found him when we got to his bed on rounds, about half an hour ago. I have no idea how long he'd been that way."

"But I just saw him on Wednesday and he was fine."

"I know. He was okay all day long. It must have happened suddenly while he was lying in bed. The patient next to him thought he was sleeping."

I was, after all, a doctor. Possible causes of death should have been flying from my tongue—pulmonary embolus, massive coronary, ruptured aneurysm, et cetera, et cetera—and there were appropriate clinical questions to ask. But nothing of the sort happened. Dully, without being able to think of anything more to say, I thanked Furman for all he had done for my father and then hung up, still both incredulous and not. Hardly a Moses, Meyer Nudelman had seen the promised land of his son's future, but he would never enter it.

I could not imagine a world without my father. I had never gone anywhere but that he was a constant presence in all that I did, even though I may have had no awareness of carrying him within me. He permeated my thoughts, though I did not always know it. His call seemed always about to come, pulling me back unwillingly from my escape. This one time, which in that brief moment I naïvely assumed would be the last, Si Furman did it for him.

My father had always held me back by his needs and his power over me, while at the same time propelling me forward in my haste to increase the distance between us. And now he was gone from my everyday life. I was free of him; the insistent inner wish had finally come true, and I was sorry for it—and relieved. Something of me could fly aloft without looking back. And something else of me wished he still lived.

But even as I began driving toward 2314 Morris Avenue an hour later to be with Harvey and arrange for the funeral, I knew that I would never really be free of Pop. He would always find a way to summon me to him.

Afterword

It is a most miserable thing to feel ashamed of home. There may be a black ingratitude in the thing and the punishment may be retributive and well-deserved, but that it is a miserable thing, I can testify.

CHARLES DICKENS, *Great Expectations*

For too many years—while he lived and after his death—I have been consumed with the futile effort of trying to rid myself of Meyer Nudelman. Still, during much of the attempted escape, I have sought to come to terms with my father, even stumbling and falling along the way. Weakened and made frail, my shoulders stooped by an illness whose emotional torments succeeded in mimicking his physical ones, I have seemed in those dreadful hours to become him. At the worst of times, fearful thoughts have had to be burned out of my brain with great jolts of electric current. I have required much help.

I will never know the cost of being Meyer's son. When midway in life's circuitous journey I found myself entrapped within those dark and tangled woods, I should not have blamed him for my loss of direction; my father was without a compass, and he, too, had missed his path. The choices I had made and the directions I had taken to lead me into the morass were mine alone. The blundering attempts to loose myself from the thickets were also mine. But unlike him, I did at last find my way out. Even my bad choices were not enough to prevent my ultimate choice, which was to resume the voyage, and make it in peace.

As a child in the synagogue on Yom Kippur, I would stand alongside my father in tremulous awe as we intoned the ancient formula before the heavenly decision is made as to who shall be at peace and who shall be tormented: *But penitence, prayer and good deeds can avert the severity of the decree.* The Hebrew word translated in the prayerbook as "penitence" is *tschuvah,* whose literal meaning is "return." I have owed Meyer Nudelman recompense for the ravages inflicted on his years, and for my inability to perceive his unhappiness. It is by returning to memory and to my father that I have sought to comprehend my own severe decree against myself, the guilt and sickness whose ravages are not to be forgotten. My quest has been to perceive what he really was.

Understanding has come but slowly. It has taken me overly long to reach this stage of the journey, when I am finally able to look back and see so much of him. With full awareness, I have sought to be what he could not be. But I have not been able to deafen myself, through the years, to the siren call of its opposite: dark, enfeebling seduction luring me to make myself what he was, and it has sometimes unmanned me. In seeking to escape him, I have drawn closer, and now at last I know that the closeness can be good. I have been trying to find his way in America for him, and for me. There is no end to it.

A Note About the Author

Sherwin B. Nuland, M.D., is the author of *How We Die: Reflections on Life's Final Chapter,* which won the National Book Award in 1994. He is clinical professor of surgery at Yale, where he also teaches bioethics and medical history. In addition to his numerous articles for medical publications, he has written for *The New Yorker,* the *New York Times, The New Republic, Time,* and the *New York Review of Books.* He writes a regular column for *The American Scholar* entitled "The Uncertain Art." Dr. Nuland and his family live in Connecticut.

A Note on the Type

This book was set in Monotype Dante, a typeface designed by Giovanni Mardersteig (1892–1977). Conceived as a private type for the Officina Bodoni in Verona, Italy, Dante was originally cut only for hand composition by Charles Malin, the famous Parisian punch cutter, between 1946 and 1952. Its first use was in an edition of Boccaccio's *Trattatello in laude di Dante* that appeared in 1954. The Monotype Corporation's version of Dante followed in 1957. Although modeled on the Aldine type used for Pietro Cardinal Bembo's treatise *De Aetna* in 1495, Dante is a thoroughly modern interpretation of the venerable face.

Typeset by NK Graphics, Keene, New Hampshire

Designed by Johanna Roebas